For The Sake Of America IV

Sheila Holm

John 10:27. *My sheep hear My voice, and I know them, and they follow Me.*

Romans 8:14. *For as many as are led by the Spirit of God, these are sons of God.*

Acts 5:38. *And now I say to you, keep away from these men and let them alone; for if this plan or this work is of men, it will come to nothing 39 but if it is of God, you cannot overthrow it – lest you even be found to fight against God.*

For The Sake Of America IV

For The Sake Of America IV

ISBN: 9781076165282

Unless otherwise indicated all scriptures are taken from the
New King James version of the Bible.

Web Site: hisbest4us.org or sheilaholm.org

Twitter: @SheilaHolm

Facebook: HISBest4us, Sheila Holm Christian Author

Printed in USA by HIS Best Publishing

DEDICATION

To the Father, the Son and the Holy Spirit for the depth of truth revealed in these days is beyond comprehension.

To President Donald J Trump for his willingness to proceed forward in faith after committing to take on the depth of evil our nation has been encased within for many generations.

To Rodney Howard-Browne for releasing the global truth so all who have ears to hear and eyes to see the plan of the enemy which is unfolding in the world, to realize how to pray and take action for the sake of souls in these days.

To Mark Taylor for standing firm in truth while sharing the exact words from our Father to the believers around the globe in these days.

To Carol Marfori, for prayerfully seeking deep truth & editing!

To LT, And We Know, for releasing Serial Brain 2 decodes so citizens across our nation will personally realize the reason to 'learn the comms' and 'trust the plan', to personally know that they know how to do everything they can to retain liberty & freedom.

To Dorothy Spaulding, Channel 49 TV for introducing me to Mark Taylor and for Mark's introductions to Christopher McDonald, McFiles, Shannon, Omega Man Radio, and Sheila Zilinsky media, for the opportunity granted to me to reveal the truth to believers on your programs aired throughout the world during these unique days in HIStory.

4

Table of Contents

Introduction: Father Knows The End From The Beginning

This book was not going to happen.

The first book was not going to happen. Facts were being shared with everyone who showed interest in taking action! Then, while I was attending a church service a woman I was not familiar with tapped me on my shoulder and told me, *You have to put the information GOD has given to you in a book so the people can read it, chew on it ...* Quickly, I thought I was getting off the hook by telling her, *I've already written 11 books ... I doubt another book would help ...*

Then, the church service began and GOD convicted my heart before the praise team was able to begin! He confirmed that He gave the word to her, to share it with me due to my resistance.

Wow. It was a very, very long church service!

The first book was written within days. It flowed due to the depth of information GOD provided during days in each area of Georgia.

The book was released on Yom Kippur in 2016.

The second book was NOT going to happen even though a reader for 'book store sales' read the book and told me the first book leads to a second book. I was shocked. The book was 'all inclusive' and I was ready for what is next on GOD's schedule for me!

First auto accident in my driving career happened that week ... no car ... trusted it was time for me to move on.

That night, our Father convicted my heart and before I realized what I was doing, I was 'making a deal with GOD', *You promised a flow that would begin in Georgia. I'm not seeing a flow so there is no reason for another book!*

The next morning, GOD provided three clues within the hour. Within ten minutes of making a call to the gift shop, I threw a few things in the rental car (provided through the auto insurance company) and I was on my way to view the flow of oil direct from the word, flowing from the bible since exactly seven days after the inauguration of President Trump.

The second book was released on Yom Kippur 2017.

Grateful the books were released and I could finally focus upon the books I 'set aside' for more than a year.

The relief I started enjoying was actually 'short lived' because the reader for 'book store sales' offered to pay me 'in advance' for the third book! I told her I was not able to accept any money for something I am not going to write. She smiled and told me I would be writing the third book because the first two books lead to the next book.

GOD and I had a conversation. I filled the moments with the plans for the 'other books'. GOD did not interrupt. He merely listened.

While I was in Macon helping the widow I assist each month, I told her the 'funny status' shared by the reader since I trusted there would not be a third book!

Within a couple of hours, we were at the local orphanage thrift store. We save our plastic bags from stores during the month and provide them to the thrift store for their customers.

The moment I walked in, a new manager was excited and pointing while he walked over to us and said, *It's you …* while I was explaining, *I have not met you … I do not know you …* he ignored me and continued, *You were wearing what you are wearing right now. You were in my living room, standing on the other side of my coffee table.* Again, I told him, *I have never met you and I have never been in your home.* Still ignoring me, he said, *It was you and while you were standing there I saw the design of three flags ... waving on my coffee table ... and that does mean something to you.*

My widow friend was laughing so loud, I'm not sure if he said anything else about the vision. GOD prompted me to share a few specifics and it was great because the manager understood the truth our Father was revealing in the books.

Many delays after it seemed like the book was ready to be released in the summer so I could proceed with 'whatever our LORD is planning for me'.

The third book was released on Yom Kippur, 2018.

The first copy was handed to the reader for 'book store sales'!

While I was enjoying the days working on the books I 'set aside', I was attending church one morning when a man leaned on the back of the chair in the row in front of me while he told me, *Woman I have a bone to pick with you.* He was so serious when he said, *I'm not getting any sleep and it's all your fault.* I thought there was something wrong until he explained the status to me, *I see a gem so I keep reading. Then, I realize I am 6-7 pages into a chapter and it's late so since I want to see how it turns out I decide to finish the chapter before I go to sleep. But then, I peek at the beginning of the next chapter and I see more gems and before I know it I am 6-7 pages into that chapter ... so, I'm not getting any sleep.*

Immediately, our Father prompted me to introduce him and his beloved to a few people in the area.

They were so excited to meet everyone, they decided to move to be with their family instead of visiting them once in a while.

When I shared the information with the reader for 'book store sales', she said, ***Don't be mad at me. There will be a fourth book.***

What?

Why would she be saying this to me?

Before I could ask, she explained her statement, ***GOD has revealed significant revelations to you and the next book will include the revelations which will wrap up the facts shared so far ... people need the information so they will know how to take action ...***

Invited the couple who used to have difficulty sleeping after they met me, to attend a bible study with me in South Georgia and to meet my widow friend in Macon.

When they heard about the thrift store manager and what GOD revealed to him in a vision regarding the third book, they thought it would be interesting to meet him.

Within moments, the manager was so comfortable meeting them, he walked us outside and stated the SAME REASON as the reader for 'book store sales' shared with me, a confirmation from our Father so I would know why there will be a fourth book.

In between the two confirmations, on Palm Sunday weekend while I was at an event, I asked our Father if He wants a fourth book, I would have to know what the title will be. In His sense of humor He merely said, *For The Sake Of America IV.*

Surprised me so much, I had to laugh.

Personally, deep inside, I knew that He knew I was asking about the sub-title because they have surprised me each time He reveals them. Interesting to see how they proceed to gain momentum as the series unfolds. He has clearly provided deeper truth for each book in the series. Book III was so deep, I trusted the series was complete. I declared, again, it was the final book.

The more I prayed to know His plan, GOD confirmed it was the right time to begin talking about 'being in action to save the nation'.

Father drew my attention to the scripture regarding 'go forth and disciple'. **Matthew 28:19-20.** *Go therefore and make disciples of all the nations, baptizing them in the name of the Father and of the Son and of the Holy Spirit,* **20** *teaching them to observe all things that I have commanded you; and lo, I am with you always, even to the end of the age.* **Amen.**

It is all about the people!

Evil, the plan of the enemy, wants to eliminate us!

We aligned with the idea of the 'nations' being separate established countries around the world.

Nation merely means a people of a language, a culture.

The invasions happening in America are above and beyond what the nation is prepared to take on because the people invading are not interested in speaking the language or becoming part of the culture 'on the land'.

They declare they want to be here 'for the blessings' while they do not adjust to the language and the culture. The unresolved issues are stacking up decade by decade due to not being addressed. Instead, government forms, and that even includes the extensive voting documents, are printed in multiple languages.

As a body of believers, we have, over time, separated ourselves from the issues, calling it 'separation of church and state' without understanding what the term means. We have departed from each other, divided due in large part to denominations. Decade by decade, many (too many) believers merely want GOD to fix it or take us home!

Due to division, we become more divided and the 'get it handled' day to day isolates us from true believes and we do not realize what is going on ... why are millions of people entering who are not interested in learning the language or the culture?

Therefore, after ancestors 'paid the price on the land' and we have continued to send missionaries for many generations to take the truth to the nations, the people around the world, we are now at a 'tipping point'. We have reached a critical point in time in our nation when the number of people who do not believe the word, do not choose to align with believers in truth about the kingdom and therefore, they have no knowledge of how we became a blessed nation. The 'I want it my way' people appear to out-number faith filled believers in many regions of our nation. When believers 'believe they are out-numbered' so it 'feels impossible (feelings LIE) to stand firm in truth to proceed and protect our culture and our language', we are forgetting the truth: LIES are used to open the door for the enemy! It is the world kingdom that works hard to convince us 'it is only acceptable to be politically correct (only use world terms) vs. stand firm in truth and remain biblically correct'. Many are shocked about this status but, it is not new. We allowed this to happen!

Personally, I was deeply blessed when Bill and Gwen Morford shared a special gift, *Fulfillment of Prophecy, The Life Story of Eliezer Ben-Yehuda.* Eliezer was told by his doctor that his life was ending very soon. Eliezer asked our Father what he should do with his remaining days. Our Father confirmed the assignment: *Update the ancient Hebrew.* Main quote shared about the assignment given to Eliezer, *The two things without which the Jews will not be a nation: The Land and the Language.*

What do we need to know, to do, to retain our nation as

ONE NATION UNDER GOD?

Align with our Father to gain His wisdom.

Then, we can become as wise as the serpent while we remain as gentle as doves.

We were informed how to become as gentle as doves and in the process we became a silent majority, without obtaining knowledge, **Hosea 4:6.** *My people perish for the lack of knowledge,* or studying to gain understanding regarding the symbols used by the enemy so we can recognize the evil plans and proceed in our full power and authority as ambassadors for the LORD Christ on earth!

Now, we are shocked to find out the enemy appears to be controlling everything about our options in life and to communicate our opinions with one another. It causes many to believe there is no hope for change or a future. Enemy plans!

Example: New laws are actually being passed which fine legal citizens up to $250,000 (New York) for using the term illegal alien because of an agenda proposed to be politically correct, so ALL must use their term illegal immigrant (to merge all illegals into the immigrant status) because the term was widespread and accepted.

When the laws 'of the land' are NOT based upon truth, the population is being controlled by the government; we have tyranny. When we stand firm in truth, knowing we are to be the voice, the leadership, retaining a government serving We The People, to live 'free on the land' in Liberty & Freedom.

This lawless, unjust status in America may seem brand new to us, but it has formed into this structure steadily for the past decades!

In the mid-1990's, I was sharing details about the invasion of illegal aliens into California and by that time, political correctness was taking over. Therefore, even attorneys were ignoring the fact the term immigrant is legal and the illegal aliens are foreign nationals who are not legally being processed to grant rights to live in our nation.

Entertainment attorneys reviewing my film and TV projects wanted me to change the term to 'match the term being used by the news media, illegal immigrant, since the term illegal alien is a term which may offend some and therefore, cause my project(s) to not be funded'. Nearly 25 years ago, we were already at the tipping point of the agenda to force political correctness and we did not challenge the status! I stood up for the true term … no funding...

It was a shock and yet, a request which was easy to answer!

Immigration is a legal process.

Illegal is not a term to be used with immigration.

They are foreign nationals, illegal aliens until they choose to enter into the immigration process and actually become an immigrant in America.

If I went to their nation and I tried to assimilate as a 'citizen', gain rights or benefits, I would be refused, referred back to America because I would be recognized as an illegal alien.

It is the same as calling evil (illegal) good, and good (restraining illegals from entering illegally) evil!

Isaiah 5:20-21, 23. *Woe to those who call evil good, and good evil; Who put darkness for light, and light for darkness; Who put bitter for sweet, and sweet for bitter! 21 Woe to those who are wise in their own eyes, and prudent in their own sight!*

23 Who justify the wicked for a bribe, and take away justice from the righteous man!

Those who operate with evil intent or plans become vocal, as we are witnessing today, because they have proceeded within their plans, their agenda, for a long time and they were allowed to continue without disruption. We have allowed the exact same agenda in many areas, including the use of their evil symbols & plans due to lack of wisdom. How does this happen? We are not training up the children to have a relationship with our Father.

They became bold by 3/22/1980 when they erected the Georgia Guidestones. Many across the nation are experiencing lawlessness and injustices which are based upon the declarations of the evil enemy upon the Georgia Guidestones. One key example is # **7. Avoid Petty Laws and Useless Officials.**

17

In these days, we are finally beginning to realize the depth of evil shared within the sources of news media by consistently changing the news from truth to lies! Then, merely repeating the lies knowing they are only stating FAKE NEWS, daily, hourly, while constantly repeating the same lies and words to appear to be sharing the news as the truth.

Therefore, the news media, as in social media, are able to control ALL of the media structures created globally and spread LIES 'with a simple click of the mouse' on the world wide web (the title takes on a whole new meaning now). This is how it has become so easy to control ALL people, by controlling ALL news media sources globally.

Reason?

To control the population in a 'group think' (mob) manner.

Why?

Once a population is controlled by what they hear 'in the news' and 'within social media outlets', they will ONLY accept and then align with & repeat the LIES as truth to all who think they can trust the media.

Then, the EVIL expands into MOB RULE without more effort by the liars because the evil plan, aka, 'Master Plan' of the enemy, unfolds without resistance because the people are controlled without realizing it because they trusted 'the news' to be truth.

What did we do?

We participated with EVIL by passing on the exact same lies (stating them and then, merely by clicking and sending lies within a controlled communication system of social media, etc.) to all of the friends who trust we are sharing the truth so they click and share, and so it goes, on & on & on & on & on.

Humorous that the EVIL plan of the enemy is now called: **The Resistance.**

What are they resisting?

<u>Any thought which does not, or any person who does not agree with them</u>!

We have allowed this!

France became famous as **The Resistance** during WWII, with the intent to preserve France!

It is NOT the same purpose in America today. **The Resistance** in America is growing as a resistance mob, resisting everything about our elected President, resisting everything about a Christian nation & a praying President.

What does this mean?

We are at war. Critical to wake up and realize we are at war!

<u>The war is against us, any people of faith, any believers</u>.

It was always the 'Master Plan' of the enemy.

Nothing has changed from the beginning of time!

The enemy uses the same reason and the conflicts, and wars are based upon the same facts: *Elimination of the believers, globally.*

Many are actually stating, *"I have joined the resistance..."* Even the candidate of the other political party in America who became the 'other candidate' on the ballot for President in 2016, the candidate who did not win the election. Yes. She made this exact same claim to extensive applause during her first media interview after she lost the election: *I have joined The Resistance!*

Problem: We were not 'trained up in the way we should go so we would not depart from it': **Proverbs 22:6. Train up a child in the way he should go, and when he is old he will not depart from it.**

Instead, generation by generation we have compromised with the enemy at each phase of the process which is causing believers to be shocked regarding the status of our nation today.

Resolution:

1 Repent.

2 We must seek wisdom direct from our Father!

PRAY! II Chronicles 7:14. *If My people who are called by My name will humble themselves, and pray and seek My face, and turn from their wicked ways* (REPENT), *then I will hear from heaven, and will forgive their sin and heal their land* (RESTORE).

This status is not new!

Within 300 years of the Crucifixion and Resurrection of Christ, everything abruptly changed. Christians 'felt better' because the persecutions and crucifixions were curtailed when Constantine was 'credited for legalizing Christianity'.

However, what actually happened 'under his declarations as Emperor, honoring the venerable day of the Sun with Sunday closure of all shops in the marketplace and only allowing farm work to produce crops on that day each week' changed the path for Christians from that day to the current day.

Constantine worshiped the sun god, Baal.

Constantine aligned all dates of worship with the pagan calendar.

Paganism was not new. It was the 'religion of the world' since Nimrod, a direct descendant of Noah!

Remember:

ONLY two kingdoms!

We were sent to be an ambassador 'on earth' so it will become on earth as it is in heaven!

Nimrod actually declared he traveled to the sun and became the sun god. Yes. He was prideful! Greed also set in because he wanted power over ALL of the people.

The people in that day were also forming The Resistance!

Constantine was merely 'one more emperor following Baal'. The emperor rings confirmed their allegiance to the sun god and their coins. issued for centuries, included an image of the sun god!

Some of the bizarre declarations of Nimrod and his mother are provided within my book, *A Wake Up Call: It's Restoration Time.*

Grateful the research was arranged by our Father for the truth to be shared! Personally, it was not comfortable for our Father to repeatedly tell me: ***Don't be a Nimrod!*** until I woke up to the fact HE was telling me to research the man (not a god), his family (Noah, Enoch…), and how he was able to easily LIE to establish *The Resistance* to the ONLY LIVING LORD at that time.

The EVIL in this world is due to who is 'in and only of the world'!

Evil is not new in the world. Century by century many have become martyrs for the faith, the truth.

In June 2014, **Christian Today** article confirmed 70 million martyrs since Christ.

Satanist portrayal of Satanic days according to Wikipedia:

In *The Satanic Bible*, founder of LaVeyan Satanism, Anton LaVey writes that "after one's own birthday, the two major Satanic holidays are Walpurgisnacht (Saint Walpurga was healed many times and Christians prayed to him for intercession in order to protect themselves from witchcraft, believing this saint caused the region in Germany to convert to Christianity; celebrated April 30

& May 1; May Day – with nations promoting dancing around the May Day pole …) and Halloween." (Underlining, added)

Other holidays celebrated by members of the Church of Satan include the two solstices, the two equinoxes, and Yule (Christmas, the birthday of the sun gods). Plus, they have Satanic rituals on a REGULAR basis! Their calendar is VERY FULL of blood sacrifice and especially child sacrifice!

Sacrifices are blood, dismemberment of humans, sexual acts with 'others' and especially children, even including the loss of life and giving gifts of blood and body parts to others, as an honor, a gift held in high esteem … the list is lengthy and each one is a confirmation of the evil rituals carried out on a consistent basis from ancient days to current days!

Thought I would insert the calendar – pages of ritual dates – however, the calendar is filled with horrific rituals of human blood and life sacrifice. The list is so long and gruesome, and our Father confirmed to me, again, the focus for us is NOT upon the enemy!

Our focus is always upon our Father and His plans for us each day!

A resource is listed within the RESEARCH section of this book if you want to view the calendar.

Example: Why would our Birthday be the focus for an evil ritual? **Counterfeit plan against the exact date we are sent to earth to help it become on earth as it is in heaven!**

Critical to realize our Father formed us in His image.

He sent us, He knows the end from the beginning.

He gave us the assignment, our purpose and plan.

His desire is for life to become 'on earth, as it is in heaven'.

Realizing how important EACH of us are to our Father's plan while we are on earth is the exact reason why the effort of the enemy to use the tactics of fear, doubt and unbelief. Why? To merely distract us from our plan on earth enough to steal, kill and destroy the plans our Father has laid out before us. Plus, to cause us to think we are not able so we will accept defeat and turn to the world for support, for our income and for a plan which makes us feel more comfortable (feelings are lies, not facts) with 'how we feel personally' as our 'future plan in our mind takes over' so we will not deny the enemy's plan!

LIAR … LIAR … LIAR!

ALL of this to keep us from walking in faith and seeking the hope and future our Father has 'in store for us'!

Key facts about Yule are included in my book, **Christmas.** Additional facts about paganism rituals are mentioned, along with the merger and 'take over' of holidays:

1. Ishtar, fertility god, children sacrificed and blood used to 'dye eggs'. Her name in English is Easter. Resurrection is separate and not a Sunday scheduled celebration on the Hebrew calendar.

2. Christmas date is the actual date of the birth of the sun gods, except Dionysus so they moved his birthday to December 25. Christ was born on Feast of Tabernacles, it is the time when all gathered in Jerusalem and that is why the taxes were collected at that time, as confirmed in the same scripture reference which is interesting. A key scripture to confirm we are 'no longer Gentiles and not to do as the Gentiles do (pagans, those who do not know the truth), do not cut down a tree, ornament it with silver and gold ... is outlined in **Jeremiah 10.**

More facts about these dates are included within my books, specifically: *A Wake Up Call: It's Restoration Time* and *Christmas.*

If you are asking yourself, *Why did God send us to such an evil world?* a question we receive often within emails submitted through the web site contact form ... the answer is clearly provided to us: *We are here for a purpose and plan our Father assigned to us, for us to fulfill upon during our 'time on earth', to go where He needs us to go, do what He does and say what He says. The truth is included in the confirmation we were taught by Christ as an example when He walked the earth. Christ also taught us to*

25

pray, knowing who we are as joint heirs, so it will become on earth as it is in Heaven.

Chapter 1   Ambassadors Sent To Earth

GOD sent each of us with a purpose and a plan, within His 'Master Plan' and it was His plan and desire for us to live abundantly and prosper. So, what happened?

We are 'on earth' where the kingdom is evil.

We have allowed steps to be taken against us.

We are at war. This was AND still is a spiritual war.

Critical to wake up and realize we are at war!

The war is against us, any people of faith, any believers.

It was always the 'Master Plan' of the enemy.

Nothing has changed from the beginning of time!

After speaking at an event and seeing how believers want a word of comfort more than a word of revelation of the LORD, and I knew there was a lot of work to do and little time to get the job done, I asked our Father, *How can I make it simple for people because so many messages with so many interpretations are making it so complex ... Your people are being lulled into 'comfort conversations for their personal issues' ... how can I make it simple for the people to know the truth?*

Father asked me to take the salt shaker in my right hand and the pepper shaker in my left hand.

He asked, *Are you the salt of the earth?*

Wow. For a moment, my thoughts turned to the scripture in **Matthew 5:13+** where we are (as believers) described as the salt of the earth unless we lose our flavor so I said, *I hope I represent You as the salt of the earth.*

He responded, *Good. When you operate in My will, you go where I ask you to go and do what I ask you to do, to say what I ask you to say, you are the salt. Everything else is not.*

Speechless.

Tears.

Father knew I was stuck in time so he said: *There are only two kingdoms.*

Simple.

Clear message.

Before I took a deep breath, our Father prompted me to study **Matthew 5: 13+** and in those moments, it was tough to deal with my thoughts: **Believers Are Salt and Light.** *You are the salt of the earth, but if the salt loses its flavor, how shall it be seasoned? It is then good for nothing but to be thrown out and trampled underfoot by men.* (Underlining, added.)

Yikes!

A lot to take in!

Then, after I proceeded upon more research for this book, I noticed through so many promptings to research 'the repeats in history' and how 'good intentions' for this nation (as in other nations) were a powerful beginning but, time after time the believers compromised and then aligned with the other kingdom. Then, life changed from liberty and freedom to lawlessness and injustices being allowed in all sections of the nation.

America is NOT the first example.

Again, it was powerful for me to ask our Father what we can do to return to Liberty and Freedom. I was deeply blessed to hear His simple reply: *I sent each one to the earth with a purpose and a plan within My 'Master Plan' so it would become 'on Earth' as it is 'in Heaven'.*

Wow! Had to let that soak in for a moment because I knew the wording was exactly how Christ taught us to pray.

However, what are we to do about it now?

Father held me while I took in the truth. And due to my request to receive a confirmation so I will know that I know I should share it far & wide, I received a photo within moments from a dear friend in San Diego.

Caleb

Her grandson, Caleb, just walked into their home.

She was prepared to take a picture this time, because she knows his pattern: Each time Caleb enters for a visit, he immediately walks over to the bookcase and picks up her copy of *For The Sake Of America II* so gingerly, it confirms he understands the message even though he is too young to read a word of the content. The book was released because our Father revealed 'the flow of oil direct from the bible in North Georgia' with three clues provided within the hour, after I cried out to see the flow our Father promised the prophets when believers repent for the atrocities in our nation, **II Chronicles 7:14**, the blessings would flow in Georgia and then across the nation as a mighty flood *For The Sake Of America.*

When our Father blessed me with the confirmation through Caleb, He immediately reminded me of the moment when a man called from Florida and shared a prophetic word which aligned all of the past events of my life 'on earth' into one message.

Harrison, a man who knew nothing about me beyond a response from Bill Morford, the man who was prompted by our Father to translate the bible into English direct from the Hebrew: *If you want to deliver a prophetic word to President Trump, the person you should call is Sheila Holm.*

Harrison called me to deliver the prophetic word.

My first reaction was laughter as I do not have a direct connection to President Trump!

However, our Father immediately silenced my laughter when the man who knew nothing about me, beyond my name & phone number supplied, began to talk to me about my life!

The details were so specific, I knew our Father was speaking directly to me through this man as he *described my personal family status, exactly, my business dealings which were done in faith and trust while the people involved were not trustworthy, while he prompted me to BEGIN to comprehend I was NOT living the life of Job, even though all assets were taken from me at a specific point in time by those who could not be trusted. Father wanted me to know I have experienced 'and overcome' the exact circumstances, atrocities which would cripple many people for the rest of their life, keeping them from being able to overcome and be productive in their life again, at any time in their future ... and yet, our Father knew I would remain faithful to HIM because we made an agreement about my assignment before I was born ... while I was still 'spirit' ... I was willing to live a life 'like Joseph' ... to have everything taken from me ... to have no earthly, family inheritance ... to be thrown into the pit, and imprisoned ... and, what our Father wanted me to know in this moment, from Harrison, is that HE has taken my hand and pulled me up and out of the pit, HE has used the key to open the prison doors for me and HE has done all of this because I was here on earth 'on assignment' to do whatever it takes to save this nation!*

IT ALL MADE SENSE IN THIS MOMENT!

The amazing depth of wisdom shared while I was driving resulted in missing a turn within moments of receiving the call which resulted in me driving on a path SOUTHWEST instead of SOUTHEAST for 1.5 hours! Fascinating how our Father reveals so much within moments! In this same moment, He was also

32

confirming my past was in the SOUTHWEST and my future is in the SOUTHEAST (for now or from now on is up to Him), truth being revealed due to a man calling me, a man who knew nothing about my life 'in the natural'.

ALL OF MY LIFE has led me to this exact moment in time, after traveling with our Father to nearly every nation around the globe, to be prepared to take in the depth of the truth in the midst of being encased within a web of deceit 'in the world' as nations have experienced, and now, America, and then reveal the truth to the people who choose to proceed as outlined in **II Chronicles 7:14.**

II Chronicles 7:14. *If My people who are called by My name will humble themselves, and pray and seek My face, and turn from their wicked ways* **(REPENT),** *then I will hear from heaven, and will forgive their sin and heal their land* **(RESTORE).**

Wow! Everything I have experienced, it was all going to matter to people who believe and follow Christ *For The Sake Of America!*

When I went back to our Father to ask about a simple way to explain what I just found out about my life 'agreeing to the assignment before I left heaven', as I asked our Father about 'making the message simple and HE provided the Salt & Pepper lesson', it was so special to realize the truth 'in simple terms'.

When I asked about 'my huge assignment which I agreed to before I was sent to earth', HE blessed me with time and explanation, again, as in scripture:

We are formed in HIS image, representing HIM, and 'in the spirit' we each know why we are sent to earth by HIM at the exact moment in time for our assignment to be fulfilled upon during our 'lifetime on earth'.

He asked me to remind ALL believers that we knew why we were sent and what our purpose and plan was before we were formed in the womb.

Then, we arrived!

We were 'in spirit' still, when we arrived, while fewer and fewer 'in the region' knew (or used) the spirit language to communicate with us.

The 'adults' spent extensive time and effort teaching us the language of the region and 'how we are to act and talk and proceed, to be accepted in the world' while this was NOT the plan HE had for us.

This is why other babies 'still seeking those who speak in the spirit' choose to seek out and communicate together. When we 'depart, align with the language and the culture in the world' it can take years or decades to 'come back to our first love'!

Some are not able to make the re-connection 'on their own' and that is why our Father has called SOME to be pastors, SOME to be teachers and SOME to be evangelists with SOME to be Apostles and Prophets who 'together with Christ, the Chief Cornerstone' form the church.

WOW.

WOW.

WOW.

This is why it is easy for me to remind ALL who believe Yahweh that our Father does NOT love any ONE of us ONE ounce more than any other ONE of us!

Each day, praying the LORD's Prayer helps to put us on the path. We are to remain willing to repent, surrender and align together in the prayer Christ taught us to pray, to stand firm against the 'Master Plan' of the enemy.

Until we take our position, aligned with the plan, ready to fulfill upon our purpose, we are not able to impact the path our family, our region, our state and now our nation is proceeding upon.

When we are not aligned with our Father, our 'out of alignment' or 'amount we have compromised with the enemy's plan' reveals how much the 'Master Plan' of our Father is in jeopardy.

Change is not possible until we accept the truth:

1. We each have an assignment from our Father,

35

2. Father arranged the assignment with us and we agreed to proceed upon it before we were sent to earth, before we were born,

3. We each have a piece of the puzzle, a part of God's plan for us to fulfill upon 'while we are on earth', and we are critical to God's 'Master Plan' on earth so it will become 'on earth as it is in heaven'.

Truth:

He will honor our prayers.

He will never leave us or forsake us.

He does not give up on us.

We go 'off track' easily 'as humans' so it is important to NOT forsake the gathering of the fellowship of believers because we are to surround ourselves with believers and remain 'in the word and prayer, in constant communication with our Father', i.e., pray without ceasing in all situations and with all people, for our battle is NOT against flesh and blood but, against the powers and principalities (spirits)!

This is a good moment to stop, make a list of the people we have battled. Then, repent for not going to our Father to gain wisdom in how to pray for the person, stand firm against the spirits so the spirits impacting the person will be dealt with and they will be set free. We are here to help set the captives free!

Therefore, praying as we were taught by Christ will help each of us hear what we are to do TODAY so the 'Master Plan' of our

Father can unfold within our generation and be passed on to the third and fourth generation!

This is the plan set forth for us, before the foundation of the world!

Our Father simply replied, *Tell MY PEOPLE they were sent as Ambassadors to Earth NOT to represent an earthly kingdom to Me but, to represent Me as LIGHT sent into the DARK world, as Ambassadors of the Kingdom of Heaven to all people on the earth, examples to ALL who have ears to hear and eyes to see TRUTH while MY PEOPLE are observed choosing to be the salt and light on the earth, not becoming aligned with the earthly kingdom.*

Wow!

If we could journey back in time with our Father 'to the very beginning' and see His plan the way He planned it all for us from the first day forward!

Wow!

Praying we will fully comprehend our Father is the ONLY one who knows the END from the BEGINNING & it will cause us to always seek His wisdom!

The reason hind sight gives us 20/20 is that we can look back and SEE how our Father walked us through the 'minefield' on earth! With our Father's guidance & His knowledge, His understanding & His wisdom, we can walk forward on a direct path to our future, our destiny!

Trusting if we had a chance to 'personally see His plan as He planned it', we would walk in faith with Him from now to eternity!

Each day is a brand new day to 'walk in truth by faith'.

He wants to show us His plan!

He is revealing the enemy's 'Master Plan' so we can see how to take our position and Trump the plans of the enemy NOW!

Remember the words in the Preamble to our Constitution, a document formed by the Native American Indians, the Pilgrims, Puritans of the Faith, and our Founding Fathers who knew the 'schemes of the enemy and the impact upon government structure' and knowing this, they chose to sacrifice ALL to form a government built upon Biblical Principles and Laws so the people could retain Liberty & Freedom: *We the People of the United States, in Order to form a more perfect Union, establish Justice, insure domestic Tranquility, provide for the common defense, promote the general Welfare, and secure the Blessings of Liberty to ourselves and our Posterity, do ordain and establish this Constitution for the United States of America.*

We are at the critical time of making our choice.

We are at the 'tipping point' where those 'in power' are crying out for the 'antique document' to be changed, modernized to be brought up to date.

Did you know they were already in the planning stages for a new Constitutional Convention, because they intended to rewrite the constitution at the time of the 2016 election?

We can choose which path!

We can walk forward in faith with Him, believe 100% that we are each an Ambassador from Heaven and command the truth in full power and authority exactly as the Holy Spirit is revealing it to us 'in the moment'.

Praying it will be the desire of We The People to proceed forward in truth.

Praying we will want to proceed in life based upon knowing His truth for there is ONLY ONE TRUTH! And, as believers, we know that we know He is the Way, the Word and the Truth!

The depth of revelation is so amazing in these days. Our Father is revealing the depth of the enemy's 'Master Plan' against us so we will realize once and for all that we are joint heirs with Christ and the earth is NOT our home. Knowing we were sent as Ambassadors 'to earth, so it will become as it is in heaven' is our assignment!

We have work to do 'on earth' for it is clear that we are surrounded by evil and yet, we must remember that we are NOT fighting against the 'people / the flesh & blood' (even though we are crying out the name of the person being affected by the enemy, the evil spirit) but, we are fighting against the powers and principalities (evil spirits operating within people)! We are here for their sake, for souls are at stake and saving the souls is our goal!

What is the difference between the body and the soul?

The body was 'built by God' in the garden, remember?

The body is the physical 'portion' we see when we view a person on earth.

The reason we pray 'all may be well with your soul' and we share the greeting one to another 'peace be with you' is because when Christ resides in our heart, we are at peace. Any unforgiveness, or unrepented issues gather and impact the well-being of the soul. We are to repent and forgive so all may be well with our soul. If there is a question about what we need to repent for or what we need to forgive, a good option to begin the process is to ask our Father: *What is the enemy holding against me?*

Then, pray the prayer of repentance for whatever our Father reveals! If you want a brief outline to help you, contact us (contact form: hisbest4us.org) and we will provide the outline attached to a response email. You will enjoy the freedom you feel after the prayer!

If you are asking yourself the question: *The battle belongs to the LORD, right?*

Yes. I agree, the 'battle is the LORD's battle'!

We are here as HIS Ambassadors 'on earth' to proceed 'boots on ground'.

Ask Yahweh what to do 'in the moment' for we represent Him!

If you are asking yourself the question: *The battle is for the LORD to fight so why would we proceed?*

These battles are NOT for us to fight 'in our human power'. Believers who have 'tried it on their own' were unable to accomplish the task. This is why they would want to convince you to 'walk away - just let it go – God will handle it – God will 'fix it' – it is not something we should worry about'.

The enemy knows how to deter us from our destiny!

Remember: EVERYWHERE we are weak, Yahweh is STRONG! Then, once we have done all we can to stand, we are to stand firm even before we put on our armor with our Father as our rear guard, we stand.

Truth: It becomes easier to comprehend the ACTUAL status when we realize 'we are the Ambassadors of Christ', joint-heirs and we are to operate in full power and authority guided by our Father and Christ through the direct guidance of the Holy Spirit.

Then, the battle is proceeded upon by us in GOD's full power & authority!

NOT in front of GOD, each step we take is directed by GOD!

This is when we shall see VICTORY!

This is when we shall declare VICTORY IS OURS!

Often, people want me to 'take it on' and yet, they are concerned about being involved due to the fact 'prayer includes the name of the person to be addressed'.

The prayers, the process of the battle, are NOT focused upon the NAME of a human to bring harm to them! The name MUST be stated for the TARGET of the enemy's plan is through that person!

The battle is against the powers and principalities, the spirit(s) we must deal with to resolve the matter, the issue, the upset which is being caused 'in the in-between' to divide and conquer US, the FELLOWSHIP of BELIEVERS.

It is NO DIFFERENT if the spirit is doing all it can to divide the people 'in the immediate family' in your home, or 'in the family of the LORD, the believers in the fellowship' or 'within a family gathering in a church building'. The spiritual battle is the same.

When we 'walk away' because we do not want to be considered 'speaking against the person' we do not understand our position in the battle or what we are battling. Remember, the battle is not against 'flesh and blood' (the person) it is against the spirit(s) operating in the person. The enemy is focused upon destroying the person. We are here to help the person, to disciple them, to free them from bondage, so all may be well with their soul!

What I am describing is critical to understand because we are 'at choice' when a situation reaches the point where it must be dealt with and to effectively 'deal with it' we require the assistance of the Holy Spirit to 'take on the entity(ies) involved in the battle'!

Remember: Enemy tactics of fear, doubt and unbelief will be used to steal, kill and destroy you … you are NOT to enter in 'on your own' … invite the LORD into the battle!

This is why it is important to NOT allow people who operate in fear, doubt and unbelief to surround you during the battle!

Father desires to reveal His counter-plan to us, personally, because He knows exactly how the person is being destroyed due to lack of knowledge: **Hosea 4:6.** *My people perish for the lack of knowledge,* understanding, keen discernment to know the difference between the voice of the Holy Spirit and the counterfeit, to gain the wisdom from our Father and reject the enemy's plans and schemes.

Important to learn the voice of our Father for HE confirms if we do not know HIS voice, 'in the last days the counterfeit will sound like our Father'!

Father help us begin each day in praise and thanksgiving for we know You reside in the praises of Your people and we choose to be aligned with You, to be Your people and walk in faith, guided by You through the Holy Spirit!

The good news is, we are NOT of this earth and we are NOT to allow the plans of the enemy to cause us to compromise with the enemy in these days. Our Father's plan is for us to prosper and live an abundant life. We have to decide where we will stand! We have to know we will be able to respond: *Me and my house serve the ONLY LIVING LORD!*

While we put on our armor to do the battle of this day 'on earth' may we remember:

We are seated in heavenly places, for we are here ONLY as representatives of the ONLY living LORD, our Yahweh over all, while living on this earth as one of His Ambassadors sent direct from Heaven.

It is our privilege and honor during each of our brief, temporary days 'on earth' to serve the ONLY LIVING LORD.

Knowing this truth, we are ready to 'take on' the devastating atrocities which have unfolded upon the earth and seek the Father's wisdom to know our position, our place to stand so the kingdom on earth will become 'as it is in Heaven' for the people who are not aware of the truth, yet, to witness our faith, our stand as an Ambassador of the ONLY living LORD.

As a dear friend and sister in Christ says often, *It's not about a good presentation, it's ALL about being a demonstration!*

Christ demonstrated.

Grateful to labor in the field with you during these unique days in HIStory, for many who already believe are not aware of how to take their position, to fulfill upon their purpose within the 'Master Plan' of our Father in these days.

Bless you for taking on the challenge, for 'this time in HIStory was chosen specifically for us by our Father when he established the foundation of the earth, and therefore it is our shift' as Ambassadors on earth, armed with the knowledge that 'lives are at stake'!

46

Chapter 2   Faith Monument

The title changed in recent time to a unique title: **National Monument to Founding Fathers** and sometimes it is referred to as the **Founding Fathers Monument.** The 'new title' does not align with the monument intent or purpose because it was absolutely established by Congress for the citizens to live by faith, with the bible being our guide to proceed per the four pillars of life as defined on each corner of the monument: Morality, Law, Education & Liberty. The monument was paid for by the Founding Fathers & Congress, as were the first 10,000 bibles printed in America for a copy in each home, school & church.

The Faith Monument is a guide to help all citizens live by faith and gain wisdom from our Father and through the bible, the word, guidance from our Father, wisdom we are to depend upon and wisdom we are to use while training all future generations to retain our liberty and freedom. This is the specific structure of the faith monument.

In the history books, the truth being passed on from generation to generation by the Native American Indians is missing. They were able to successfully live abundantly upon the land under Divine Law for more than 2000 years before the Pilgrims arrived.

Faith Monument, Erected 1889

Faith: Located at the top of the monument, pointing up to our Father in Heaven while holding the bible.

The four pillars at the foundation of the **Faith Monument:**

1. Morality is holding the Ten Commandments in her left hand and the scroll of revelation in her right hand. At the base of the throne are the engravings: **Evangelist** and **Prophecy.** She has no eyes. She looks inward because truth and liberty must be in us before it will show up within the nation.

2. Law founded upon the bible, the source of truth as the Pilgrims **General Laws** confirm: *...by how much they (the laws) are derived from, and agreeable to the ancient Platform of God's Law.”* The two carved items under the throne where **Law** is seated represent **Justice** and **Mercy.**

3. Education is holding an open book of knowledge, the Bible. Her throne has two carvings: **Youth** receiving instruction and **Wisdom** represented by a grandfather who points to the bible while standing on the globe, confirming both the parents and the grandparents are to teach the youth from a Biblical perspective. She is wearing a **Victory** wreath for focusing the youth upon the truth and the way to proceed in their life, resulting in the *training up of children in the way they shall go so when they are old they will not depart from it* as confirmed in **Proverbs 22:6.**

4. Liberty is seated with a sword in his hand. He is prepared to protect the family and retain liberty. Two carvings are shown for **Tyranny** and **Peace.** The images clearly confirm why the Pilgrims, Puritans, were known as the *Parents of America, the Republic* confirmed by the Founding Fathers.

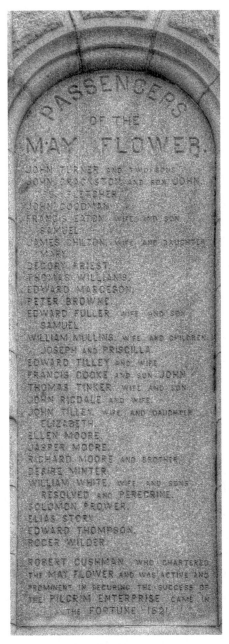

Mayflower Passengers

Only 42 of 107 arriving on one ship survived the first winter.

Quote by William Bradford

On the Faith Monument, a special quote from William Bradford speaks to the depth of faith, knowledge, and wisdom in the people we refer to as Pilgrims or Puritans of Faith:

Thus out of small beginnings greater things have been produced by His hand that made all things of nothing and gives being to all things that are, and as one small candle may light a thousand, so the light here kindled hath shone unto many, yea in some sort to our whole nation, let the glorious name of Jehovah have all praise.

Bradford focused all praise on the Hebrew name of our LORD, the Father, Jehovah our Yahweh, Yah or Y-h (vowels not used), the praises to the one true and only living GOD (G-D). Hallelujah means 'praise be to Yah', God be praised, the worship of Jehovah / Yahweh, Yah.

With everything based upon the Word, the Bible, and the exact details being provided to keep our nation free and all people living in liberty, how could a blessed nation return to the traditions of pagan worship, again, and repeat the pagan rituals of Christmas and Easter, and allow the perversion of specific dates to honor the saints, i.e., Halloween lies instead of All Saints Eve or All Hallows Eve, celebration on the Eve of All Saints Day? *Father forgive us!*

Instead of following our Hebrew calendar which includes the structure the LORD put in place, we denied the truth after receiving so many benefits from the Christian standard set by Christ, our Yeshua Hamashiach, who followed the Hebrew calendar and truth was demonstrated again by Pilgrims / Puritans.

Over time, what did we do?

We aligned with stories, lies we heard without researching the facts to know the truth. When truth is revealed, it is hard to comprehend the depth of the stories because truth becomes a shock after decades and generations of lies!

Facts shared were not based upon truth. We merely heard lies repeated generation to generation and then, without question, we repeated the same lies as though they were great stories, and we did this again and again, generation to generation. Then, we diligently participated in and wanted generations to 'do better in

53

the world than prior generations'. Now, we wonder how the current generation appears to be 'so far off the mark'.

Who did this to them? We did!

It's a sad status for us today, especially since the Hebrews were granted the land and lived free on the land under Divine Law for more than 2300 years on the land Christopher Columbus (actually a Jewish man, from the lineage of Colon in Italy) named America.

When the bible was translated into English and it included the Apocrypha (1611 King James), the Pilgrims knew the truth and they knew they were willing to sacrifice everything to come to this land of America our Father arranged for HIS people.

The Pilgrims arrived with a 500 year plan, a plan established in truth for our success, our freedom and liberty as a people until at least 2120! It was a plan which worked beautifully for less than twenty years. Sad!

The 'new people' made 'new treaties' with the Native American Indians and they changed everything about daily life and cemented the fate of the tribes of Israel in America with the Native Indian Removal Act. This was done after the homes and land were taken away from the Native American Indians and the land was placed into deeds with personal names assigned 'for a fee paid to the new government'. Similar to plans in recent years resulting in legal citizens not able to hold on to their homes and land while foreign nationals, undocumented people, are given benefits and rights, plus assistance in obtaining 'the American dream', help which is not available for citizens. More facts in my book: *Nation Restoration.*

Divine Law

Divine Law was ignored and erased, causing generations to not realize the truth: *We are not here to gather assets in our name for our sole use, we are only here on earth for a brief, temporary time, to help life 'become on earth as it is in heaven'.*

LORD forgive us!

Would be nice to know what it would be like if we would have continued upon the 500 year plan! We would have bypassed debacles created by removing Native people from their homes and land and we would still be proceeding upon the plan for another 100 years, united together as believers on this blessed land!

LORD forgive us!

We are realizing now why the Native American Indians shed tears as they departed. They did not lose their faith in the Creator, the Holy Spirit, the tears were for the 'walking dead' who did not realize the enmity they were creating between the people and the Creator, the Holy Spirit, our Christ and Savior, our Father.

LORD forgive us!

There is a strong push for a new, Constitutional Convention to establish a new Constitution, to replace the 'outdated, antique'.

More repentance and prayer required!

Founding Of America: Constitutional Convention

As the Founding Fathers were leaving the Constitutional Convention in Philadelphia, Mrs. Powell asked a simple question: *What have you given us Dr Franklin?*

She received a simple response from Benjamin Franklin: *A Republic, if you can keep it.*

The plan to retain America as a Republic is confirmed in our founding documents and the Pledge of Allegiance: *... and to the Republic for which it* (the flag) *stands.*

What is the difference between Republic & Democracy?

A Republic government is of, by & for the people. Each citizen has rights as a sovereign citizen.

In a Democracy, rights are granted to and secured by majority and the majority rule can be real or perceived (fake news) which often results in becoming mob rule while the majority do not participate or speak up. It has already happened: *The silent majority.*

When the people fear the government there is tyranny,
when the government fears the people there is liberty.
Quote by Thomas Jefferson

The constitutional convention is important to Georgia with a key person participating who would make a huge difference within the future plans from Macon, Georgia to Moravian Falls, North Carolina. The exact location God identified *For The Sake Of America* when GOD released the word to the prophets.

Important to realize the connection between these details of pushing the Indians south of the Ohio River and then, deciding to sell the reduced acreage of land belonging to the Native Indians to the cotton plantations coming south from North and South Carolina into Georgia. This is the exact location of what GOD confirmed to the three prophets in the vision which made the location so critical to America. They were crying out for America when our Father confirmed that He has positioned angelic vortexes over Macon, Georgia and Moravian Falls, North Carolina *For The Sake Of America.*

There is a strong push across America now by groups who are united in their belief that another Constitutional Convention needs to be held as the Constitution is 'out-dated' and therefore, they want people to believe it has to be changed. The only changes which would be helpful would be to legally remove the amendments added, amendments which changed the intent of our constitution.

Truth is Truth

There are no versions of the truth!

57

The truth was given to us to carry on before we established America as a nation in 1789, the same truth the Native American Indians (people of Israel origin) successfully passed on from generation to generation for more than 2200 years. The sad news is that America was being directed to proceed upon a different path within two decades. A few examples:

1. Removing the Native American Indians, knowing they were the lost tribes of Israel; depicting them as savages within TV & film projects, while not revealing they were doing what they could to protect their family and land.

2. Forcing them to walk to Oklahoma from the East Coast, after the Cherokee won their case in the Supreme Court.

3. Forcing reductions of acres of land again and again and again due to 'land rush' options arranged by the federal government, even within Oklahoma.

4. Sending Ministers & Missionaries to prison, to serve in hard labor camps. due to knowing the truth and defending Native American Indians who were doing

everything possible to express & expose the truth in Georgia.

5. Repeatedly removing Native American Indians from their homes and their land, enslaving, auctioning and lynching the men; placing children in a type of foster care, with adoptions by people who enslaved them, breaking apart the families and keeping the future generations from hearing and knowing the truth about their heritage and lineage. Many families confirm: Foster grandfather, great-grandfather and great-great grandfather, going back five generations. This fact is 'outlined in scripture', a fact which is now a key to the EVIL 'restructuring of America' plan!

Father FORGIVE US for we DID NOT KNOW and there is so much more we DO NOT KNOW. Thank you for NEVER leaving us or forsaking us for we KNOW there is much more which will be revealed in the next days and months. We praise you for keeping your hand upon us while we continue to seek your truth, walk forward in faith and DISCIPLE as you direct from this day forward!

Chapter 3   'End Game' Symbols Positioned

ONE SYMBOL:

Medical – Sports – Travel – Trade & Thieves - Messages to the other gods, Underworld & Border Crossings.

ONE SYMBOL! A symbol ONLY used in America!

The enemy uses symbols to communicate, to control and manipulate.

This is why we were warned: **Matthew 10:16-20.** *"Behold, I send you out as sheep in the midst of wolves. Therefore be wise as serpents and harmless as doves. 17 But beware of men, for they will deliver you up to councils and scourge you in their synagogues. 18 You will be brought before governors and kings* *for My sake, as a testimony to them and to the Gentiles.* **19** *But when they deliver you up, do not worry about how or what you should speak. For it will be given to you in that hour what you should speak;* **20** *for it is not you who speak, but the Spirit of your Father who speaks in you.*

What is the plan of the enemy against us today, identified within the ONE SYMBOL?

A symbol used for Medical.

It is a symbol which actually represents a Greek god over Messages to other gods, Sports & Athletes, Travel, Trade & Commerce, Thieves, Trickery, Border Crossings and the Guide to the Underworld.

Perhaps a good moment to take a DEEP BREATH, a new BREATH OF LIFE from our Father!

The list appears to align with the CURRENT CONDITION IN THE WORLD!

Nothing to fear! It's EXACTLY why we are here!!!

Are you wondering how ALL of this is related?

Well, it's all related to and through one Greek god, **Hermes.**

A god who is the basis of the medical symbol, a symbol which is ONLY the medical symbol used in America.

62

When I started the Medical Legal Evaluation corporation, I was told it was the Rod of Jesse: **Isaiah 11:1-2.**

There shall come forth a Rod from the stem of Jesse,
And a Branch shall grow out of his roots.
² The Spirit of the LORD shall rest upon Him,
The Spirit of wisdom and understanding,
The Spirit of counsel and might,
The Spirit of knowledge and of the fear of the LORD.

Plus, the wings were supposed to be the **wings of an eagle**, representing America!

WOW. However, LIES were shared! Lies which were spread far & wide and yet, the truth, the facts, are very, very different!

Perhaps they were confused but, the medical professionals told me (and I told many others) that the rod was the rod of Jesse, the staff or branch in the Ark of the Covenant which was dead but, 'it has evidence of life'. The rod 'in the Ark' is actually the Rod of Aaron, not the Rod of Jesse. Discernment required!

A lesson learned:

Important to research what is being shared before sharing it!

Again, without my knowledge, it was a lie being shared as the truth by the very medical professionals who were thrilled I was going to use the medical symbol as the logo for my corporation.

Sad to say, I proceeded based upon human input and zero wisdom from our Father! A LOT happened in my life due to making the choice and proceeding with the corporation while I trusted the corporation would be 'my future' ... 'my retirement' ... but, all it was 'in truth' was my plan! I had pulled my hope and future back from God's plan and held it 'in my hands'.

Yikes! I was re-directing my life without any input from our Father!

Tough to hear people say 'God allowed all of this horrible stuff to happen to you'. Not true! At the time, I was upset. Many moments were spent 'blaming God' without realizing the impact of entering into hope deferred. Grateful God did NOT give up on me! It took a while for me to realize, what was happening to me was NOT orchestrated in my life by our Father!

It seemed like the life of Job with the enemy sifting every aspect of my life, daily! However, what I was 'doing to impress', while 'making so much money for me and my future', seemed like it would be a status which would be forever real! I easily accepted & trusted it was going to 'be my future'.

Thank the LORD, He chose to take my hand and lift me up and out of all of it and show me the bigger picture, the real assignment for me in these days!

Why? Because I actually 'forgot my assignment', the purpose and plan I agreed to 'in the spirit' before our Father sent me to earth to help it become on earth as it is in Heaven! I agreed to do whatever it takes to save this nation. Hours of repentance turned into days!

Man did not and still does not have the answers!

I accepted input as though it was truth but, I was NOT told the truth!

Medical symbol: ball & wings at the top of the rod are the symbol confirmed by the American Medical Association, the **Rod of Hermes**:

Meaning of the **Rod of Hermes is** based upon the question, *Who is Hermes?*

Greek god per Ancient Greek religion:

1. Messenger of the gods,

2. Over trade and commerce,

3. Over thieves and trickery,

4. Over travelers,

5. Over sports and athletes,

6. Over border crossings, and

7. Guide to the underworld.

Well, it took a few moments for the depth of the lies told to me, lies I accepted as truth, to realize they were LIES – a lot of time for the truth about the lies to 'sink in'!

Reading and re-reading the list ... while glancing over the rest of the words which state the medical community was confused at the end of the 19th century and beginning of the 20th century and in their confusion, they began using the wrong symbol as the medical symbol in America.

Yikes!

They were not aware of who the author of confusion is!

They put the plan in motion and did not seek the wisdom of our Father!

Each word made it harder to take in the depth of the deception put in place in America, because there are significant, distinct differences between the **Rod of Hermes** meaning and the significance of the **Rod of Asclepius** the REAL medical symbol used in the rest of the world; everywhere else IN THE WORLD!

The medical symbol around the world is completely different, because the **Rod of A**sclepius is merely a simple straight rod, often called a staff, and the meaning is completely aligned with the purpose since Asclepius is the ancient Greek god of healing and medicine and his rod or staff represents medicine and health care to this day.

So, what do you think?

Immediately, seeing the definitions, I think about the staff which became the serpent when Moses and Aaron entered the court of the Pharaoh.

Father prepared Moses & Aaron. **Exodus 4 & 7.**

In Exodus 7:8-13. Then the Lord spoke to Moses and Aaron, saying, **9** *"When Pharaoh speaks to you, saying, 'Show a miracle for yourselves,' then you shall say to Aaron, 'Take your rod and cast it before Pharaoh, and let it become a serpent.' "* **10** So Moses and Aaron went in to Pharaoh, and they did so, just as the Lord commanded. And Aaron cast down his rod before Pharaoh and before his servants, and it became a serpent.

11 But Pharaoh also called the wise men and the sorcerers; so the magicians of Egypt, they also did in like manner with their enchantments. **12** For every man threw down his rod, and they became serpents. But Aaron's rod swallowed up their rods. **13** And Pharaoh's heart grew hard, and he did not heed them, as the Lord had said. (Underlining added)

Then, our LORD sent the plagues.

Were the people choosing the symbol confused by choosing the wrong rod or were they aware of the difference between the two gods? Was the choice based upon confusion or was it a choice based upon a specific plan designed against the people?

To me, the choice appears to be one more part of the **'100 year plan' against us** a renewal of the evil, given direct to people like Albert Pike and Alice Bailey (amongst others) through their 'bracelet communications with the enemy'.

Medical – Sports – Athletes – Crossing Borders – Trickery – Thieves ... Reason appears to be direct alignment with the plan of the enemy because of the steady increase in pharmacy use. Today, the meaning of pharmacy is merely where drugs are made and disbursed. Not the truth!

Reason why I am wondering and researching layer by layer: We are experiencing symptoms which are 'not known to physicians' even within the current medical structure! More and more truth being revealed today confirms we did not know the truth about athletes, travel (trafficking of children, and especially young women), trade (tariffs were set up to NOT charge a tax upon the people and their income or production), etc., or border crossings!

LORD forgive us!

After resting with our Father about all of this, I researched layers of medical information and the various meanings of

68

Pharmacy before current day interpretations of merely making and dispensing medicine.

By the late 1300's:

Medicine. From the old Greek term pharmakeia, meant the use of drugs, medicines, potions, or spells; poisoning, witchcraft; remedy, cure.

Pharmacist. One who prepares drugs, a poisoner, a sorcerer from pharmakon.

Pharmakon. In philosophy and critical theory, the term has three meanings: remedy, poison, and scapegoat, while the term is also known to refer to a drug, a poison, a charm, a spell or an enchantment.

Ah, the time required to let all of this sink it ... well, it took a lot longer due to the influences of the enemy in so many areas of daily life.

During prayer, our Father reminded me that the believers lived many, many years without going to physicians, taking medicines or potions prepared.

In ancient days, they went to the fellowship and prayed!

The depth of this information gave me a lot to 'ponder' for a 'long time' because looking up the 'true meaning' of terms was not a main focus in my life.

Wow! Our Father protected me from so much that would have affected my soul. It took a while to come back to the point to be able to say 'all is well with my soul'.

Thanking our Father for helping me with the transition from merely 'accepting statements as truth' when people who appeared to have more knowledge, declared their truth was the truth. TAKE IT TO THE FATHER!

However, with knowledge (remember, our Father said in **Hosea 4:6.** *My people perish for the lack of knowledge*), we need to gain understanding so we will walk in truth, in wisdom with our Father!

Once we gain wisdom, in relationship with our Father and guidance of the Holy Spirit, we can truly take a fresh breath of life from the Father and observe what is happening because it truly seems like the evil plan of the enemy against the people of America 'through the chosen medical symbol' (also relating to sports, athletes, travel, border crossings, trade & thieves, and guide to the underworld; through the evil rituals, abortions and complete disregard for life of believers) is exactly what we are watching unfold in these days!

This moment in time is a great moment to 'take a new breath'!

Why? (TAKE A BREATH FIRST)

The wings on the Rod of Hermes are the wings of a cockatrice.

Plus, the double snake on the rod is ONLY on America's medical symbol! The medical symbol I was provided for the logo:

In America, I admired the gold pins worn by people licensed in the medical profession, so I used this symbol within the logo, It appeared everywhere, on the business cards, the stationery and all communication with all sources.

Personally, I did NOT see the true structure of the rod of Hermes, the **caduceus** which is the name of his symbol and the American medical symbol!

It is the ONLY symbol using the Rod of Hermes, two snakes (the two-snake caduceus design has ancient and consistent associations with trade, eloquence, trickery, and negotiation) and the wings of a cockatrice instead of the eagle wings, as I was informed by medical professionals.

The **caduceus** is actually in the form of two snakes wrapped around a winged staff with carvings of the other gods.

71

Everything about Hermes was 'winged'!

He was son of **Zeus and Pleiad Maia**, a fact which will be even more significant in the second portion of this unique chapter.

Hermes was known as 'the divine trickster' who supposedly traveled freely between the mortal and the divine worlds, perhaps because he typically wore a winged cap or helmet and winged sandals.

The difference in the symbol of Hermes is due to the wings being the wings of a cockatrice.

What is a cockatrice?

A rooster.

A bird with his head on a small, slender dragon type of body which has a royal crown appearance on the crown area of the head.

A male bird which actually lays eggs that hatch as serpents.

Isaiah 14:29. Amplified Bible (AMPLIFIED)

Rejoice not, O Philistia, all of you, because the rod [of Judah] that smote you is broken; for out of the serpent's root shall come forth an (cockatrice) adder [King Hezekiah of Judah], and its [the serpent's] offspring will be a fiery, flying serpent.

Isaiah 11:8. Amplified Bible (AMPLIFIED)

And the sucking child shall play over the hole of the asp, and the weaned child shall put his hand on the (cockatrice) adder's den.

Isaiah 59:5. Amplified (AMPLIFIED)

They hatch (cockatrice) adders' eggs and weave the spider's web; he who eats of their eggs dies, and [from an egg] which is crushed a viper breaks out [for their nature is ruinous, deadly, evil].

Wow! While reviewing the research prepared for my personal hours and days of repentance for being involved in the medical industry without realizing what I was entering into, nothing within the medical research included the name cockatrice. In fact, internet searches stated the cockatrice was fiction and did not exist.

Now, while I was updating all of my research, I was directed to a new Cockatrice computer program developed and released in New York, New York.

That's right! Cockatrice has become a business name for an open source, multi-platform program for playing card games on your table or over the internet, a program openly marketed to families.

Coincidence?

While researching the company to find an address in New York, since I was curious to find out if it is also housed in the UN building, I was shocked when the research immediately re-directed my search to a 1903 New York Times article about the Cockatrice. When I clicked to view the article, the NYT wanted me to subscribe to their paper. I was not able to take a screen shot of the page from 1903 but, feel free to search for an address for the title of the program in NY, NY to see what will be revealed. The lower right corner of the New York Times article page showed an ad for three new novels with the first one titled: Master of Warlock.

The logo for the program appears with the ads for it, as of 2013 and the new program Beyond Horizons was released this summer, in June 2019, and the revised version of the main Cockatrice program was released in July.

Another Deep Root:

Another deep symbol.

Same lineage of Greek god Zeus but, a different plan.

What is the root?

Pythia.

Who is she?

Daughter of **Apollo.**

Who is Apollo?

A twin to Artemis, a son of **Zeus & another consort, Leto**.

Link to another Greek god, another son of Zeus.

What is the meaning of her name, Pythia?

It is a name derived from Pytho/python, and pytho actually means the **sickly sweet smell of the decomposing body of the monstrous python after it was slain by Apollo.**

Pythia was recognized as the high priestess of the temple of Apollo at Delphi, a town originally known as Pytho.

Pythia was widely known as the Oracle of Delphi with 'seekers of her godly wisdom' from many governments and regions.

Why was Pythia the recognized oracle within and beyond Greece?

She once disclosed the exact type of turtle soup the king was eating at the time of the counseling appointment!

Who is an oracle?

A person who provides counsel in the temple, prophetic predictions, precognition of the future as inspired by the gods, recognized as a form of divination.

When were words given by the oracle?

On the 7th day of the month.

Why were they given on the 7th day? The number seven was the number most associated with the god Apollo.

What is Delphi?

Delphi is a town, a town originally called Pytho.

Home of the **Temple of Apollo,** later known as **Temple of Delphi** and later recognized as **Temple of Diana of Ephesus!**

How did Delphi become well known?

It became the center of the region due to the **Oracle of Delphi, Pythia.**

Pythian Olympic Games Apollo Ancient Coin

The United Nations (UNESCO, UN Educational, Scientific and Cultural Organization) has declared the location as a World Heritage Site. What does this mean? The site is now protected by International Treaties. Therefore, the site is legally protected under the Law of War under the Geneva Convention.

So, what does another Greek god have to do with the current status of the nation? We merely need to look at the status of the government and the church, for both are equally encased within a web of deception.

Lets start with the meaning of the name once again: What is the meaning of the name Pythia? Pythia is derived from Pytho and it refers to the sickly sweet smell of the decomposition of the body of the monstrous python after it was slain by Apollo.

There is huge reason this information is so important:

Python or Leviathan or Jezebel, similar spiritual process.

Python: Restricts/constricts, chokes, strangles/suffocates; kills.

Leviathan: Strangles or chokes; kills.

Jezebel: Control, manipulate; witchcraft, divination; kills.

Why is this so critical?

This root is part of the **Pythian** secret society, kept secret from the Masonic order structure which was established in America at the same time, during the Civil War, and both were formed by men who lived 17 miles from each other in Massachusetts before they established the societies. Pythian supposedly began in Washington, DC within a year of Rathbone arriving and working at the Treasury department; Pike due to being in Macon, Georgia, the location which was going to be the new government headquarters after the Civil War, a man who resigned (due to arrest) during the Civil War.

77

Both men established the organizations with the exact same plan: *Structure and control of each community across the nation.*

Pythian secret society was supposedly established with the first lodge in Washington, DC in 1864 with many lodges built as castles across America. The society was the first to be granted a charter and later, national credibility by an Act of Congress in 1913. Facts are confirmed in articles and in the information on web sites established and maintained by the secret society while the Congressional Bill granting funding to this secret society is still secret; not easily located within lists of Bills passed by Congress.

Why is the Congressional Bill important?

The societies funded by this secret society: Red Cross (global) & American Cancer Society. Evil plans being revealed in this year link to the funding and actions of the organizations funded.

The title of this secret society: **The Pythian Society.**

The plan: Identical to Masonic, structure each community.

Remember, the significance of 1913 within *For The Sake Of America* Augusta chapter?

1913: President Woodrow Wilson opened the door! He confessed on his death bed; regretted what he did to the nation!

Everything was changing from Republic to Democracy due to Wilson. We pledge to the Republic for which our flag stands.

CHANGE TO DEMOCRACY / PROGRESSIVE

The change to Democracy and being recognized as Progressive people with Progressive plans for the future was the master plan for the New World Order!

This plan, as with these secret societies, expanded into 'a global plan' of control. The societies are a factor in the plan to change ALL nations from Republics to Democracies.

In fact, missionaries were sent out to make the nations proceed exactly as the United States, to help each nation proceed with the same structure in their nation as the global societies changed the structure in America.

While I traveled 'without an extra coin or tunic' our Father revealed missionaries helped nations to add both an Internal and Property revenue office, even when the nations were Kingdoms with a monarchy in charge vs. a representative government structure. Shocked as I traveled nation to nation and witnessed this truth up close and personal.

These plans were promoted within the nations exactly as they were promoted and believed within the body of believers to be the best structure for our future. Each generation has followed the path of the controlled 'plan to change' from a blessed nation to a nation controlled by a monarchy whether representative or not. It has all been done, in the government and in the church, to align us with the One World Order.

Prior generation to the Federal Reserve and IRS journeyed to America as immigrants from many nations and traveled to states with the nation as pioneers. They were granted 'no tax' on the property when they pioneered a piece of land in America. Are you seeing a similar, nearly exact, yet different plan unfolding today?

The critical time frame of 'changing the plan' in our nation aligns with the Presidency of Woodrow Wilson to President FDR, a man who considered President Wilson as his mentor. The two men were clearly directed on the same track controlled by the same deep state (shadow government) families of the Federal Reserve and IRS (both entities are not government agencies) and the re-structuring of the government also changed the structure of the church. Requirement of 501c3 registration. Over time, restrictions upon religious organizations and churches have increased while the restrictions upon non-religious charities & foundations have not realized the same scrutiny.

A conflict of 'Separation of Church and State'.

This Progressive plan changed our national structure and the body of believers aligned with this plan in large part due to believing America is a blessed nation while not realizing the alignment would result in 'depending upon the government'.

Now, whether the message still seems subtle or blatant, children are told their family members will not be here forever but the government will, so it is important for you to know you can always depend upon the government.

The first time I heard this, I was shocked and thought I should meet with school officials.

In the midst of my upset, our Father merely gave me a reminder message: *When you were hearing it in school, you did not say anything to counter the message ...* tears flowed.

It was subtle. Hind sight is truly an option to gain a 20/20 view of what was happening back then. If we did not feed back the same message the professor 'believed in' within the papers, our grades would reflect how much our opinions differed from the professors.

A subtle message to 'align with the professor's opinions to succeed', a message which continues within career choices and it has become more pervasive decade by decade in each generation.

It is confirmed in our current status within the church, also. We have a hard time challenging opinions, also known as sharpening each other as iron sharpens iron. This status has resulted in many within the fellowships departing from trusting their future is safe in the hands of our Father.

Instead, believers are supported for personally figuring out their future, all plans 'on our own' which means we are proceeding separate from our Father instead of asking our Father for HIS wisdom about HIS plan for us. Because we were not supported in being aligned with and discipled to hear the truth direct from our Father since HE is the same yesterday, today and tomorrow. we were guided to 'make our own future plans', 'focus upon our personal success', while supported by family and friends to learn how the world does business so our life will be 'better than the prior generation'.

This is how each generation has departed further and further from our Father, without realizing the depth of deception involved in the world plan which actually intended to move us further and further away from the plans our Father has laid out before us. This has been the focus of the enemy's plan, generation by generation for more than 100 years.

We can change this status!
Christina is proof!

June 2019. Twenty year Anniversary of meeting Christina.

In June 1999, Christina was four years old. When her parents asked her what she wanted for her birthday, she said she wanted a new tambourine to praise the LORD because her tambourine was getting old. They purchased a new tambourine and trusted the old one would be thrown away. However, Christina was told by our Father to leave the old tambourine in the church because He was sending someone to the church and Christina would know who to give the old tambourine to when they entered the church.

It was an amazing day in Camarillo, California at Jubilee Church in 1999, when Pastor Steve Dittmar informed the fellowship that the church has the funds to pay the bills and if the people want to give to the church, they can, but, if the Holy Spirit is prompting them to do something to bless someone, the church will take a break to let them do what they are being prompted to do. Men ran and obtained objects to add water and wash the feet of their wives, people gave funds to specific people in the fellowship along with words of prophecy being shared everywhere.

Then, a Dutch Reformed mother and daughter were sitting behind me. The daughter, a four-year old, handed me a piece of paper with the same drawing of my farm as I experienced being in the glory at four, an identical drawing of the experience which I received from children who were four-years old in each nation I was sent to during 1999. While her mother was confirming she was instructed to drive to the church that morning, I felt a tug.

Christina wanted my attention. When I turned to hear from her, she handed me her old tambourine.

While she was telling me that GOD wanted me to have the old tambourine because it would mean a lot to me, her mother joined us and explained the birthday request.

Amazing!

4/12/95 to 6/19/99, Isaiah 62:2 & 3

While 'taking it all in', I noticed Christina was wearing a pair of Dorothy *Wizard of Oz* red, sequin shoes. I asked her about the shoes and she leaned in really close to whisper in my ear, *They remind me we are never too far away from home, are we?*

In June, immediately when Christina entered the room and saw me, she immediately recognized me. Plus, she remembered everything about our first meeting, our only meeting, 20 years prior to this moment in time and we shared the exact same words this year as they were shared 20 years ago.

Christina's mother knew the depth of Christina at the age of four and I asked her to be sure to ask Christina what our Father was sharing with her each morning so she will not depart from our Father as she goes to school and proceeds with her life.

Christina is clearly as tight with our Father today as she was at four! She has completed college. She has an amazing corporate career and she focuses upon how to pray for others!

Paul Harvey Knew!

If I Were The Devil.

If you have not heard the Paul Harvey message which reveals the plans of the enemy the past 100+ years, it would be well worth the three minutes plus to gain revelation in how the enemy has operated in subtle yet effective ways: *If I Were The Devil.*

Purpose of Pythian Society?

Moral uplifting and purification of society. Seriously! They declare the society supports charitable, benevolent, fraternal and social activities. They support and fund the Red Cross and American Cancer Society and provide volunteers for both. Their national charity: American Cancer Society.

How did the Pythian Society begin?

A man from Massachusetts, Justus H Rathbone, a man who lived in Stoughton and the organization is still headquartered there, in a town 17 miles from the home of Albert Pike.

Both men became active at the exact same time: **Civil War.**

Who is Justus H Rathbone?

Independent research about the society or the founder, a man who is credited with founding the non-sectarian, fraternal organization, is not easy. Their sources provide the only information.

In fact, the book on *Pythian History* by William D. Kennedy, Chicago, was supposedly published by the Pythian Publishing Company, 1904. However, attempts to find the Pythian Publishing Company do not result in obtaining a business location or address. Unique businesses are registered in the Pythian buildings and names of business people are linked to those addresses. However, finding a source to cross-reference facts is not easy.

Biography per Wikipedia of Justus Henry Rathbone (October 29, 1839 in Deerfield, New York – December 9, 1889 in Lima, Ohio) was the founder of the international fraternal order of the Knights of Pythias. He graduated from Colgate University and attended Carlisle Seminary. He was a music composer and actor. In 1863 he moved to Washington D.C. as a government clerk in the United States Treasury Department, where he founded the Knights of Pythias on February 19, 1864.

Rathbone wrote the ritual for the Knights of Pythias which is based on the mythological friendship of Damon and Pythias, while he was a school teacher at the Eagle Harbor Schoolhouse, in Eagle Harbor, Michigan.

So, based upon these facts, where did Rathbone obtain the information to establish an international secret society?

When was the society supposedly established?

Pythian Society was supposedly established in 1864 with the first lodge in Washington, DC, with Rathbone only moving to DC, to be a clerk in the Treasury Department in 1863. In fact, Rathbone credits an extensive investigation of the society by President Lincoln and states the acknowledging the benefits of the secret society. How did Rathbone become known and connected within months in order to have the Pythian Society thoroughly investigated by President Lincoln?

Everything about the claims are doubtful, especially since Lincoln knew the word of God. Scripture confirms nothing is held in secret except the good which is held with the Father!

Luke 8:17. American KJV. *For nothing is secret, that shall not be made manifest; neither any thing hid, that shall not be known and come abroad.*

Jesus confirmed he did not speak in secret.

John 18:19-20. The high priest then asked Jesus about His disciples and His doctrine. **20** Jesus answered him, *"I spoke* *openly to the world. I always taught in synagogues and in the temple, where the Jews always meet, and in secret I have said nothing. 21 Why do you ask Me? Ask those who have heard Me what I said to them. Indeed they know what I said."*

NOTE: The Scottish Rite Masonic Temple structure was established in America, in New York in <u>1864</u>, also. The first temple was established in Macon, Georgia in <u>1864</u>, also. Civil War was being fought at the same time: 1861-1865 and Macon was the location of the supplies for the war and it was designated to become the new location for the government.

Remember Albert Pike?

He established the first Scottish Rite Temple in Macon, Georgia and he expanded the plans to align globally with the New World Order plan by establishing the **Order of the Palladium** in Charleston, South Carolina, Rome & Berlin.

The order is directly linked with the Illuminati globally.

Albert Pike gathered 33rd degree Mason globally with his good friend from Italy, Mazzini, co-structuring the plan.

Pike also established and led the KKK in America.

So much more about Pike provided within *For The Sake Of America, Chapter on Macon, Georgia.*

Pike also trusted his efforts supported the development of the New World Order globally, and he declared he was the leader since his effort would result in completion of the New World Order structure globally, with his structuring of America within the same format during his lifetime. The two men, Rathbone and Pike, proceeded upon an identical plan: Deceive, manipulate and control all communities within the states by withholding the plan they were proceeding upon.

Civil War. The time frame in America history was about a lot more than 'a decision upon slavery'. And slavery was about a lot more than 'people from another country, Africa', as confirmed within this book series: *For The Sake Of America.*

People outside of Washington, DC did not realize the Central Bank of New York was demanding President Lincoln accept a loan for the war! The development of political stands in DC for the entire nation by that time in history is exactly what caused concern for the patriots.

What was 'changing' in DC by a few voices became the very reason the southern or Confederate States seceded from the Union in 1861.

After the states seceded from the union, the Civil War became a 'war to preserve the union no matter the cost'. President Lincoln declining the loan was a key turning point in his life and in the status of the Civil War.

Coincidence?

Issues we are still dealing with in the nation are exactly what the South realized when they proceeded to secede from the Union.

This is why it is critical to 'know the truth' so we will retain Liberty & Freedom in this nation.

What is the Pythian society based upon?

Rathbone declared the entire structure of the Pythian society was merely based upon being inspired by a play: *The Legend of Damon and Pythias.* The play was written by an Irish poet, John Banim. Supposedly, it is the story of two men who expressed the character traits of loyalty, honor and friendship.

What are the basic beliefs?

Pythian society members believe the teaching of Pythagoras, an Ionian Greek philosopher and the founder of Pythagoreanism, 'schooling' of the original members of the society which would make it an ancient society structured long before the Irish poet, the play or the idea proposed by Rathbone in 1864.

Who was this Greek man, Pythagoras?

He was known throughout the region as a mathematician, living on an island near Greece. When he established the school and traveled, he became a man who was recognized for his political and religious teachings.

Since Pike's plan for the secret society structure aligns directly with the Pythian Society and the structures began at the same time, I am inserting a specific section from *For The Sake Of America.*

Insert from *For The Sake Of America*

Albert Pike's Foundation of Palladium

Charleston, So. Carolina, Rome, Italy & Berlin, Germany

As the Grand Master of a Luciferian group known as the Order of the Palladium, or The Sovereign Council of Wisdom, which was founded in Paris in 1737, Pike felt he ruled the New World Order at this point.

Palladium was brought to Greece from Egypt by Pythagoras a Greek philosopher who was known for establishing the Pythagoreanism **movement** in the fifth century, and it was this cult of Satan that was introduced to the inner circle of the Masonic lodges across America. The Order of the Palladium was aligned with the Palladium of the Templars. Pike established the American headquarters in Charleston, South Carolina with additional offices in Rome, Italy and Berlin, Germany.

(More facts inserted in Chapter 4)

Symbol: The Pythian society is supposedly focused upon being benevolent while the main symbol for their order, the **Knights of Pythias**, includes a helmet, a battle shield and two hatchets, crisscrossed in front of the shield. Interesting also is the fact the upright triangle with the society symbol is within their overall Knights of Pythias symbol of three upside down triangles within another upside down triangle.

91

Counterfeit symbol? Pointing to the protection of our life by the Knights. That was the first reaction when I saw the symbol for the first time. The border around the outer upside down triangle makes their symbol 'appear significant'.

What do the letters in the upside down triangles stand for?

Supposedly the letters represent what was inscribed on swords of the Knights in ancient times.

The acronym **FCB,** the letters representing the stand of the Knights for each other and their regions are claimed to now stand for the **Pythian** motto: **Friendship, Charity and Benevolence.**

Symbol of the Pythian Knights:

The main symbol within the triangle is easier to view on the cover of the book on *Pythian History* by Kennedy.

Funding: As of 1913.

Act of Congress, a bill passed for the Pythian Society.

The Pythian Society declares all funds are disbursed to benefit the communities while they have actually built castles in nearly every state while the society states 100% of their funds are disbursed to the communities in each state. Odd that their budgets show 16% for administrative costs.

If you do a search on the internet for the locations of the society lodges / castles, you will notice an extensive number of lodges along the East and West coasts, throughout the South with a few in the Midwest. If you are near Springfield, Missouri at some point in your life you may want to tour their castle.

Plus, they are supposedly under a different funding structure supported by the Act of Congress on their behalf in 1913 which is not disclosed.

The society budget is not easily accessible from the organization or from Congress, yet, and the public information about the Congressional budget does not reveal an amount specifically granted to the society.

The society funds are declared in various articles as being directly disbursed, along with a large number of volunteers provided to both the Red Cross and the American Cancer Society while the amounts they are disbursing to these organizations are not revealed within documents they share publicly.

In these days we are finding out about the many layers, various levels of evil operating within our nation. Evil organizations also involve false charities and foundations which have 'good titles' while the true intent is the opposite and therefore, the funds are being used for evil plans and purposes.

Researching 'send us money' organizations is difficult.

Believers desire to help where and when help is required. Believers submit funds to organizations with 'good titles, names of organizations which state a good purpose' while the intentions and how the funds are used not known by the public.

The organizations have become more prominent within each region since so many are locating offices in each region, arriving with needs and believers often find it easier to 'give a little' than 'become involved'. This plan by citizens is not wrong while the problem is the world has set it up to change how believers become involved with needs in each community.

Plus, the world plan requires both husband and wife to work to 'pay the bills'. Schedules for the family have become overwhelming with family activities, sports and athletic events, purposely filling Sabbath, from Friday evening through Saturday evening.

All of this has divided the families, especially believers, because our desire is to align with the Father and believers are torn in making the decision to honor the Sabbath and keep it holy and also support their family in becoming involved in sports activities!

Trusting you are seeing how subtle the world plan is and how easily it has changed the plans laid out before us, especially for the families of believers. This is absolutely presented in a subtle format 'on the surface' while it is clearly the purpose of the enemy!

It is becoming very clear why our Father confirmed the undefiled religion is to **see to the needs of the widows** (without husbands) **and orphans** (without fathers) so **we can help them avoid the snares! James 1:27.** *Pure and undefiled religion before God and the Father is this:to visit orphans and widows in their trouble, and to keep oneself unspotted from the world.*

Because believers do not have 'extra time' to visit, to see to the needs of widows and orphans, they become dependent upon the world for their needs.

While traveling, I am often hosted by a widow. Each one is experiencing financial issues when I arrive, borrowing from minimal savings to break even at the end of the month. They are typically 'giving to causes sound like good causes' because they are not able to assist personally due to their age and health. Helping them by providing facts about the organizations mailing letters and calling with requests for money every month.

It is disturbing, in fact, appalling, to hear the intense 'needs' the callers (Christian based organizations or not) want the widows to contribute to them and especially when the widow has not mailed a payment for a month or two. The callers increase the intensity when the widows share the truth, the reasons why they do not feel they can contribute during the month.

Typically, the callers will not end the call until they get a commitment to receive at least a few dollars each month. Sometimes, the calls come to the cell phone numbers of the widows while I am taking them to a grocery store or to lunch since they do not have a chance to eat out, and the callers call right back if the widows say they are not able to talk at that time. The callers know the widows will be faithful in sending the amount they agree to send so they remain on the call until they obtain the commitment, the agreement to send monthly money.

Because of working with the widows on these issues and providing the truth about the organizations, especially Christian based organizations, depending upon them for their monthly funds vs. our Father being their supplier, their provider, the widows have pulled back from mailing any checks in response to the letters and calls requesting money.

Now, I have many testimonies of the savings and checking accounts showing income 'remaining' at the end of the month which is greater than their retirement pension and social security payments. Grateful!

Praising our Father with them for our abundant life is due to being separate and set apart from the world. We are NOT attached to or affected by the plans of the world!

Father forgive us for only focusing upon being as gentle as doves, becoming a silent majority, accepting man's plans as the truth and depending upon the solutions offered in the world.

Thank you for helping us learn how to gain your wisdom direct from you so we will become as wise as the serpents for we realize now how the serpents have deceived the structure of our fellowships and our government and they have expanded their territory while we remained silent. Thank you for blessing us with YOUR TRUTH!

We thank you in advance for wrapping your arms around us, and revealing your truth to us so clearly we can hear you even when you whisper, for we desire to align with you & take back ALL the enemy has stolen from us! We declare the truth of the seven-fold return as promised in Proverbs 6:31. (when found to be a thief) *he must restore seven-fold; He may have to give up all the substance of his house. Satan, you are put on notice this day. Your attempts to deceive us, to use your tactics to put us into fear, doubt and unbelief will NOT work anymore! You will NOT be able to steal, kill or destroy any of the plans our Father has for us for me and my house serve the ONLY living LORD and we are protected by the blood of our Savior, our Christ, Jesus of Nazareth! Thank you Father! AMEN.*

Chapter 4   New, Simple Plan Added: *A Paper Clip*

That's right. A plan with an evil intent and agenda, a plan 'added' in this century to the evil plan established in the prior century.

The added, evil plan is merely an updated plan against believers, a plan structured by the enemy to affect our lives for all time because this plan specifically targeted America and then, the changes in other nations to reign all nations into the New World Order.

The plan was allowed by leadership in our government upon the conclusion of WWII. It was easily approved and enacted.

How? The process was exactly the same as in 1913 and 1917 with Congress and Senate eagerly voting to pass laws within days.

1913: Two amendments to the Constitution immediately upon President Woodrow Wilson's first inauguration.

1917: Then, upon his inauguration for his second term, the approval to remove the Christian Tsar of Russia, Nicholas II (family executed within weeks), and approval for our troops to enter into WWI.

WWII: Due to the immediate acceptance by both Congress and Senate of the tens of thousands of undocumented people allowed to invade our nation and immediately become department heads, entire teams and therefore the controllers of new government agencies established and funded without question.

This was allowed within months of our nation becoming bankrupt. New news to you? This is how we became 'subject' to the crown once again!

History.

So much for our President Trump to 'turn around'.

It is apparent now, the acceptance of the invasion of undocumented foreign nationals at our border by the politicians in DC is identical to what was allowed at the conclusion of WWII. Congress and Senate, with full knowledge allowed tens of thousands of German scientists, medical professionals and agents to enter our nation and assimilate within our society while the entire program was kept secret from citizens, to keep their agenda and operation 'under the radar'.

What was their agenda, their plan? *Operation Paperclip.*

Again, the scripture has meaning in what was going on! **Luke 8:17.** American KJV. *For nothing is secret, that shall not be made manifest; neither any thing hid, that shall not be known and come abroad.*

When I first received specific information about *Operation Paperclip,* the photos and facts which were researched and released in an article by an investigative report Don Nicoloff in the Idaho Observer, April 2007, I found the information interesting upon an initial scroll through the lengthy article. However, I did not realize a reason for me to read it or do any specific research on the subject at that time.

While I was ignoring the 'value' of the article, our Father prompted me to view a few videos regarding King Edward of England who abdicated the throne to marry his consort, a married woman, Wallis Simpson. Shocked how quickly I was 'drawn in'. The entire time, our Father pointed to 'what is next'. The throne going to his brother, and then Elizabeth. Again, I had no idea how it related or why it would have meaning to completing this book!

In the research of the 52 page article, I was prompted to view another video about the royal family regarding a different limb on the royal family tree. <u>Title</u>: *The Queen's Mother In Law* (**Royal Family Documentary**). Not much was shared over the years about Prince Philip. A few facts were featured over time regarding his royal background, with Elizabeth 'required to marry a royal'.

FACTS about Prince Philip:

He was from a royal family in Greece is all that is mentioned.

Nothing was mentioned about Denmark.

However, his REAL name is Philip of Greece & Denmark.

Father's name: Prince Andrew of Greece & Denmark.

Mother's name: Princess Alice of Battenberg.

Philip is NOT British but, he is from the British royal line.

How is Philip related to the British royal line?

His mother was born in Windsor Castle. His Grandmother is the daughter of Queen Victoria. Princess Alice is declared to be the granddaughter in the biography but, she is actually the great-granddaughter of Queen Victoria; her grandmother was Alice, the daughter of Queen Victoria & Prince Albert.

How did Princess Alice become a royal 'of Battenberg' and where is Battenberg?

Princess Alice is from the royal line in Battenberg, Germany.

Father: Prince Louis of Battenberg (Hesse, German royal line)

Mother: Princess Victoria Alberta Elisabeth Mathilde Marie

Princess Victoria later became Victoria Mountbatten Marchioness of Milford Haven.

Grandfather: Louis IV, Grand Duke of Hesse & by Rhine.

Grandmother (1st wife): Princess Alice of United Kingdom.

Great-Grandfather of Alice of Battenberg: Prince Albert.

Great-Grandmother: Queen Victoria.

Why is the German connection important?

ALL four sisters of Prince Philip married Nazi Officers.

In the research portion at the end of this book, the minute markers are identified within the video on YouTube so you can quickly scroll through the video to see Philip with his brother-in-laws when they attended his sister's funeral.

Evil plan 'from Germany' was larger than anyone realized!

Remember when Prince Harry attended a party in full Nazi uniform and it became a major press story throughout the world?

It was a shock. Then, the story was quickly changed to say it was merely a costume, a fact the media used to reduce the story by simply promoting the fact it was not done 'with meaning', it was only due to the young age of Prince Harry, a fact shared with the hope we would believe he supposedly knew nothing about Nazi Germany or WWII.

Evil plan 'from Germany' was larger than anyone realized!

Since the Otto Skorzeny article was part of our Father's plan for me, He prompted me to cut & paste the entire article into a WORD document and save it on my computer.

The article remained on my lap top until this year.

While I was visiting a dear widow I assist on a monthly basis, our Father prompted me to read the entire 52 pages out loud. It seemed odd but, she was very interested in the information and within the first few pages, I was captivated by the specifics. The article is in the same form as it was released with each part providing specifics which were thoroughly researched in America and in Europe.

The article includes photos and confessions of a man named Otto Skorzeny. The facts confirm the expanded evil plan against America. The first paragraph is a great summary of what has been taking place 'behind the scenes' so I will share the first few sentences: *What we are taught about history in American schools is not history, but a fairy tale. Better yet, it is propaganda designed to hoodwink an unsuspecting society about its true heritage and the treasonous acts and sabotage that were conceived in order to bring about a New World Order. You are about to learn the real identities of those who have infiltrated your nation on behalf of secret societies intent on bringing about the total slavery of mankind.*

It can appear on the surface as a 'new plan' while the plan which has unfolded in America actually appears to be a remodeled old plan, a revision of the attempt to establish the New World Order from ancient days, re-structured within secret societies by Albert Pike, societies focused upon eliminating believers while calling the societies Christian. That did not work, so it was established again by President Woodrow Wilson through the enactment of the Federal Reserve & IRS, plus, the establishment of the League of Nations which has evolved into the United Nations. The New World Order plan has remained the same for many decades!

Insert from *For The Sake Of America*: Albert Pike

Albert Pike to be Arrested; Theft of Materials and Funds.

Within months, in 1862, Pike was on the list to be arrested due to his mishandling of funds and materials; supplies missing from inventory and/or removed from the arsenal in Macon. The arsenal in Macon was specifically arranged for the Confederate States and all supplies were stockpiled in Macon, Georgia.

Albert Pike Resignation; Released days After his Arrest.

Pike resigned his position days prior to being arrested on the original charges and additional charges of illegal actions he allowed, crimes committed by his men. Pike's resignation letter was received at about the same time as his arrest. Therefore, Pike was released a few days after he was arrested.

Albert Pike After the War.

Pike refocused upon the financial and political structure to control communities, States and America through the Masonic Order. Pike spent significant time in Macon, Georgia.

Albert Pike becomes Top Leader in Knights of the KKK.

According to historians, by 1869 Pike was also the top leader in the Knights of the KKK.

Albert Pike coordinates first attempt at New World Order.

Pike was supposedly self-appointed as the coordinator of the first attempted structure of a New World Order with the help of his friends.

His right-hand man was from Switzerland, Phileas Walder. Walder was a former Lutheran minister, a Masonic leader who stated within his biography that he was an occultist and a spiritualist.

Pike also worked closely with Giusseppe Mazzini of Italy, a 33rd degree Mason who founded the Mafia in 1860. By the mid-1860's Mazzini was also the leader of the Illuminati globally.

Pike was recognized as the leader of the Illuminati in America.

The 33rd degree is the top Masonic position. Pike gathered only the top leaders globally from the list of 33rd degree Masons to proceed upon his plan for the New World Order.

Albert Pike, a self-declared Satanist.

According to the historical summary on Pike, he declared he was a Satanist. He stated he indulged in the occult. He actually confirmed that the bracelet he wore was used to summon Lucifer, with whom Pike said he had constant communication.

As the Grand Master of a Luciferian group known as the Order of the Palladium, or The Sovereign Council of Wisdom, which was founded in Paris in 1737, Pike felt he ruled the New World Order at this point.

Palladium was brought to Greece from Egypt by Pythagoras a Greek philosopher who was known for establishing the Pythagoreanism movement in the fifth century, and it was this cult of Satan that was introduced to the inner circle of the Masonic lodges across America.

The Order of the Palladium was aligned with the Palladium of the Templars. Pike established the American headquarters in Charleston, South Carolina with additional offices in Rome, Italy and Berlin, Germany.

Albert Pike Vision. Letter to Giusseppe Mazzini on August 15, 1871. Pike received a vision which predicted three world wars which would position the nations for the New World Order, the One World Government.

Pike shared the vision with Mazzini in writing. Pike did not realize Islam is the religion of Muslims. Pike referred to the people of Islam as Moslems throughout the letter to Mazzini.

Brief summary of Pike's vision; prediction, three world wars:

WWI required to destroy Tsars (Christian) Russia.

Goal: Atheist communism becomes prominent and destroys faith in other religion(s)

Reality: Tsar Nicholas II removed March 1917; abdicated the Romanov throne under pressure; Romanov family was arrested; Entire family executed during the night of July 16-17, 1918.

DUMA was established as an advisory group by and for Tsar Nicholas II becomes the founding structure of Communism in Russia under dictatorship rule of Lenin and the Bolsheviks. Russians agreed due to the promise of peace, land, and bread.

By 1922, Russian government was confirmed as a Republic.

The Union of Soviet Socialist Republics (USSR).

NOTE: A Republic form of government secures rights for each sovereign citizen. Russia was not a Republic government of, by and for the people.

WWII Fascists (includes Communists and Moslems, per Pike, actually Islamists) will battle against Zionists; Atheist Communism and Moslems/Islamists will become equal to the population of Christianity around the world.

Reality: This agenda became the global reality! American pilots, the Flying Tigers, risked everything in 1941-1942 to provide supplies to China during their war with Japan. John Birch was a global missionary from a young age. He served as an intelligence officer, a Captain in the Air Force, during WWII. John realized America supplied and defended China during the war while the American government sanctioned Japan. The attack on Pearl Harbor December 7, 1941, was a direct result of the Empire of

Japan's anger with the decisions of President Roosevelt to supply China and sanction Japan.

By 1949, the Chinese government was under the dictatorship of Mao as The People's Republic of China. However, China was not a Republic government of, by or for the people.

WWIII Political Zionists and leaders of the Moslems/Islamists will battle; both will be conquered and exterminated.

Later, with the Zionists becoming a big part of the banking system, the structure changed to target Muslims against Christians, with both being eliminated from the earth!

Plans for the expansion of Satan's agenda on earth were provided as a '100 year plan' through communication supposedly provided direct from Lucifer through a bracelet to **Alice Bailey, in the early 1900's, exactly as Albert Pike stated in the 1860's & 1870's.**

Alice Bailey established Lucifer Publishing. Then, later, after she married Bailey, a co-leader within the Theosophical Society, they were challenged about the title and they chose to re-title Lucifer Publishing to Lucis Trust. Extensive research about her history and plans was done by Gary Kah.

<u>Goal:</u> Influencing future generations by printing, publishing and distributing public school textbooks; changing and separating children from their parents by adjusting the school structure from small, local schools to larger, centralized schools, transporting children a distance away from their families, combining children in

the region into the larger schools which removes the next generation from the people and community they know.

Then, they proceeded to change the content of history and facts to influence the generations to rely more upon the government for advice and counsel than upon their family, including the philosophy that the government will always be there for the children while the parents and grandparents will not, they will all die. These statements are being shared even in the assignments of the youngest children in pre-Kindergarten schools today.

Rapid changes: A few families controlling everything!

Presidential issues with Monroe were significant and resulted in life-changing plans. The prior President, Madison, confirmed treaties to protect the land and homes of the Native American Indians. All was well until on the land until Monroe was elected.

As soon as Monroe was 'in place' all treaties established with Native American Indians were 'in jeopardy' and not honored even when the Supreme Court confirmed the truth!

Presidential issues with Jackson … resulting in the Trail of Tears.

Then, the major shift from President 'Teddy' Roosevelt who fought and communicated specifically about holding on to the structure of the Republic, that the government belongs to the people; President Roosevelt was personally challenged with J P

Morgan. Morgan was taking over the entire banking structure while President Roosevelt was on a 'duck hunt'.

Morgan personally decided, during a (manufactured?) banking 'crisis' in 1907, which banks would remain in place and which were insolvent. Status was not corrected even though President Roosevelt remained in office until 1909.

Then, in 1910, the financiers who gathered on Jekyll Island, Georgia, lied about 'going on a duck hunt' when they knew they were going to proceed with the Federal Reserve and IRS structure.

They went to Jekyll Island and met at their Millionaire's Club since they were the ONLY people who had the option to get to the island on a large barge. This resulted in only the elite having mansions on the island. The native people became their slaves. The island was 'given' to the State of Georgia and a bridge was built to the island for tourists to tour the island, enjoy the restaurants and gift shops, and see the J P Morgan mansion, etc., and yet, to this day, people speak about the separate beach which only the slaves of the elite were to use on the island.

Now, the island in Georgia where the elite gather is Sea Island. If you own property on Sea Island you would be able to drive to the island. However, only property owners and their guests can enter the gates to the island. It is obvious when the private jets arrive in great numbers. The people arriving do not cover up their identities or remove their names from their private jets. The plan was so far along, they evidently think it would not matter if people knew they were 'in the area' to make decisions which affect Americans, decisions made in secret.

Secret is how evil proceeds!

Secret is what is happening in our government today.

Transparency by our President about international affairs which should be held confidential due to those operating in secret, those who have the intentions to proceed with an evil plan are finally being identified!

What they are doing and how they are doing it is NOT NEW, it is only being revealed due to our President proceeding with transparency.

What happens when people with evil intent speak to the press?

Their 'truth' is revealed.

This is why we must know the voice of our Father to proceed as wise as the serpent, while doing all we can to remain as gentle as doves for the souls of the lives of those involved in the evil plans are as important to our father as our soul is to our Father.

Jesus did not speak in secret!

Ephesians 5:8-14. Walk in Light. For you were once darkness, but now *you are* light in the Lord. Walk as children of light 9 (for the fruit of the Spirit *is* in all goodness, righteousness, and truth), **10** finding out what is acceptable to the Lord. **11** And have no fellowship with the unfruitful works of darkness, but rather expose *them*. **12** For it is shameful even to speak of those things which are done by them in secret. **13** But all things that are exposed are made manifest by the light, for whatever makes manifest is light. **14** Therefore He says:

> "Awake, you who sleep,
>
> Arise from the dead,
>
> And Christ will give you light."

1913: President Taft was only allowed to remain four years while he was absolutely under the control of others for his decisions.

Remember the strange positioning as a Republican President to appoint a Democratic Augusta attorney, Attorney Lamar as Supreme Court Justice? It was even more bizarre decision President Taft was required to make since Attorney Lamar was no longer practicing law due to his serious health issues. In this condition, Lamar actually accepted the appointment to the Supreme Court.

Very interesting facts behind this appointment since we can use hindsight to realize the Lamar appointment was part of the plans already 'in place' for Woodrow Wilson to become the next President of America.

Wilson was credited with the Industrial Revolution while he was the Governor of New Jersey. He was being tested before he was positioned as the President! Yes, positioned!

The public was not aware that the new Supreme Court Justice Lamar was a close childhood baseball team friend of President Woodrow Wilson. The Lamar and Wilson families were very close over the years. Plus, the health of Lamar was not questioned when placed on the list to be considered as a Supreme Court Justice. More details are shared within *For The Sake Of America.*

President Woodrow Wilson, two terms confirmed due to cooperating with the plan!

The master plan of the group currently called the deep state, the shadow government or the global elite, actually became evident within days of the inauguration of Wilson as President in 1913.

First Term of President Woodrow Wilson:

Constitutional Amendments 16 & 17 were easily approved within days! The 'shadow government' was 'already in control', of the President and the House & Senate to change the Constitutional structure this fast!

Huge changes to our nation were passed by Congress and Senate which enacted the Federal Reserve, the IRS and changed the structure of the vote for Senators. Instead of States electing representatives and then the representatives selecting the two representatives to represent the State as Senators, the voting structure was changed to popular vote.

Our Republic was no longer a conversation since Democracy and Progressives replaced any mention of our Republic. The Republic is confirmed within our Pledge of Allegiance to the flag, to the Republic for which our flag stands.

Second Term of President Wilson:

President Wilson was directly involved in the forced abdication, removal of the Christian leader Tsar Nicholas II of Russia shortly after the beginning of his second term in February 1917, with the removal of the Tsar on March 15, 1917. Tsar Nicholas II was known as Saint Nicholas the Passion-Bearer in the Russian Orthodox Church from the first of November 1894 until he was removed in 1917. Then, his whole family was assassinated, executed on July 17, 1918. Interesting to know he was the fourth wealthiest man in the world at the time with a net worth of 250 – 350 billion in 1917 dollars.

Without knowing the facts, American men joined in the effort of WWI.

Immediately upon their return, Foster and Alice Bailey offered free membership to the Theosophical Society.

President Wilson was granted the Nobel Peace Prize for the Treaty of Versailles, ending WWI, without the citizens knowing his part in the plan for WWI. President Wilson is credited with arranging the removal of Christian Russian Tsar Nicholas II and establishing the League of Nations which was the predecessor to the United Nations. It was placed on our soil. Diplomats and their entourages from other nations are allowed entrance, freedoms & rights due to location of the United Nations in New York City.

Stalin in 1902, a declared atheist

Able to gain control over the people

Offered 'equality' through shared wealth

Leader after Christian Tsar was removed

President FDR formed 'warm relationship'

While Stalin ruled, 1917 to 1953, at least 15 million Christians were murdered between 1917 and 1950 according to a June 2014, **Christian Today** article.

August 22, 2019, I shared the photo and facts on Facebook and Twitter immediately after it arrived: **Received a message about an atheist this AM worth reviewing:** *Stalin was a popular intellectual, Socialist. He led protests against rich, promising ALL will benefit; equality. Continued his agenda until he took over & gave ALL people poverty & famine + 20 million were killed.*

The evil plan has not changed, century to century!

Examples of what was allowed in America:

Our President Woodrow Wilson with Congress & Senate:

1. Directly involved in the removal of the Christian Tsar Nicholas II and execution of his family within weeks.

2. Directly involved in the 'allowance of socialism', Stalin.

3. Directly involved in establishing and President Wilson credited with founding the League of Nations which is the structure of the ONE WORLD ORDER, ONE WORLD GOVERNMENT, ONE WORLD RELIGION known as the United Nations today.

4. Directly involved in changing the world 'as we knew it'.

President Franklin D Roosevelt, who called President Wilson his mentor, proceeded with Congress and Senate to fund China and Russia against Japan. This decision became the upset for Japan, resulting in the bombing of Pearl Harbor and America entering WWII.

The plan may be adjusted, tweaked or remodeled.

However, the goal is always evident and remains the same whether it is achieved through war or not: *The world kingdom is evil. The world kingdom does not want believers 'on earth' who operate directly with the ONLY LIVING LORD.*

Facts will lead you to the same control tactics and plan being revealed in ancient times as found within the current day events, especially the agenda of evil which 'at times' hidden in secret societies including the **Knights of Pythia**, and they link back directly to the same conquerors, the crusaders, **The Templars, the same** links to the Knights of Pythia. Conquering and taking captive, beheading and persecuting those who follow GOD … it has been the same evil plan for centuries.

Operation Mockingbird, Addition to *Operation Paperclip*

In addition to *Operation Paperclip*, an operation which formed the three letter intelligence agency starting with a C, there is an *Operation Mockingbird* which was also generated within the same agency. Remember the simple phrase, *a little birdie told me*?

Well, the plan expanded into the media with Director Wm Colby inserting 400 agents in the various media sources.

Why? His own testimony: *… to spread disinformation throughout the America*(n) *Media … mainstream television, newspapers and magazines.*

What does the process of spreading disinformation within the media mean?

The process undertaken within *Operation Mockingbird* is specifically identified by a term: **FAKE NEWS.**

When was he the director of the agency?

1973 to 1976, after serving in the agency in South Vietnam. He served in the Office of Strategic Services, the intelligence service formed during WWII which became the agency after WWII.

Then, William Casey was the agency director from 1981 – 1987, and he stated the confirmation of the same goal in his first year, 1981, *We'll know our disinformation program is complete when everything the American public believes is false.*

Today, this is why our President and those 'in the know' refer to the **FAKE NEWS** sources as **The Mockingbird Media.**

NOTE: The invasion of 'undocumented people', whether anyone calls them illegal aliens, foreign nationals or merely illegals, has been a steady flow the entire time we have been a nation. Those who entered the nation 'with evil intent' did not want the Native people, the believers or Christians to 'remain on the land'. The invasions have been steady and increasing in greater numbers since WWII, due to *Operation Paperclip,* and it has been allowed to continue and expand with EACH WAR, Korea, Vietnam, and the Middle East. Entire communities of people from other nations.

Figures are staggering for just the three letter agency portion of the 'invasion of undocumented people' from Germany is quoted as 55,000+ SS agents immediately entering our nation after WWII.

The battle we are in now about illegals is not a new battle!

It is a battle 'in the eyes of the people' now, ONLY because we have a leader who is willing to stand firm against ALL, especially those in the structure of the government who have allowed these invasions and changes to our Constitution and our laws, changes which will not protect the citizens, the ONLY people with rights 'on the land'.

More facts about President Wilson, WWI and WWII, which expanded the evil plans, etc., are shared within the original book in this series: *For The Sake Of America.*

More facts about the impact of the 'invasions allowed' since the 1970's and 1980's are within my book *Nation Restoration.*

The 55,000 + at the end of WWII were undocumented, their stories about their birth, school and family records were false and their records in their country were expunged.

Therefore, they were assisted in being allowed to proceed.

In fact, they became heads of departments which were newly formed in our government after WWII.

How did we become entangled in WWII?

President Franklin Roosevelt (FDR):

President FDR credits President Wilson as his mentor.

How are they similar?

They were both 'positioned' and aligned with war plans.

America was funding China against Japan.

Trusting you can imagine right now why Japan became so upset about America, pilots agreed to sacrifice their lives when they bombed Pearl Harbor.

The attack on Pearl Harbor became the reason Americans agreed to enter into WWII.

Actions taken have placed us in war mode for the entire 100 years since President Wilson, and the war plans have resulted in 'regime changes' globally.

Sharing these facts because of the actions taken by President Wilson and President Franklin Roosevelt opened the door to economic changes with the Federal Reserve 'notes' vs. currency, and proceeding with an expensive war based economic plan which has placed our nation deeper and deeper in debt, a door which was still wide open and not recognized as 'invasions, never ending wars and significant debt' until the election in America in 2016.

Luke 8:17. American KJV. *For nothing is secret, that shall not be made manifest; neither any thing hid, that shall not be known and come abroad.*

What changed in America due to the election in 2016?

CURSE REVERSED.

We have an opportunity NOW to change the EVIL plan by operating in TRUTH in these days!

What was 'hidden from the legal citizens' was known only by key believers who remained strong in their faith, many positioned within our military, and believers who left the silent majority and became patriots willing to take action steps and share truth after questioning and researching stories which do not appear to be the truth, and especially believers who would not compromise with the plans against citizens within our military and intelligence services.

What have the believers realized?

The wars from the Civil War to WWI, WWII, Korean Conflict which includes as many soldiers stationed in Korea today as it did in the 1950's, Vietnam which was a war President Kennedy was not going to enter into based upon military advisers. However, upon the date of his assassination, an Executive Order was signed by President Johnson immediately placing our American soldiers in Vietnam. The wars have been planned and they have continued while filling the war zones with American soldiers! Why???

Then, President Nixon opened the door to China and took our currency off of the gold standard, as advised by a man who has become well known around the world, a man born in Germany. The adviser held key positions in our government (NSA & Secretary of State). After he held the positions, a well known woman who was born in Europe held the same positions. Now, those positions are finally realized as positions in our government which were seriously compromised, the National Security Administration and the Secretary of State positions.

Plus the fact our currency has not been backed by gold since the decision was made in the early 1970's to take us off the gold standard. Our currency was operating in fiat, petrol based currency.

At the same time as the loss we experienced in Vietnam, beyond the tens of thousands of lives, resulted in taking on of refugees from Vietnam which included members of Asian gangs which we were not in a position to deal with. It was also the beginning of the process of invasions into America by people from other nations, thousands and then millions of people each year ... far beyond family members of those who arrived as refugees.

Why is this being mentioned? President Nixon was advised by a member of secret societies to take each of these steps.

All of this was completed within one segment of time within one generation. Therefore, it overwhelmed people, communities, the families, the economy and the financial structure resulting in changes to communities, schools for non-English speaking people and cultural changes in each region.

Operations established against legal American citizens were not realized as they changed region to region. If a citizen was harboring or transporting an illegal alien or foreign national who was not 'proceeding through the immigration process', the citizen was detained and charged with a crime. The people who were foreign nationals involved in the same actions were not detained or charged, they were released.

Significant evidence about these changes and how people from other nations have been treated when they break the laws of the land vs. how citizens have been treated is found within my book *Nation Restoration.*

The two specific laws added for Identity Theft, a crime regarding the theft of the Social Security Number as ID of legal citizens since it is used to gain credit and therefore credibility, is exactly what the illegals, the foreign nationals, have used for decades 'to establish in America without being an American'.

When they have been in the country for a specific amount of time, or they move to another state, they move on to a different ID. They are not apprehended or dealt with because they have to pass the threshold for the authorities to deal with the crime, an amount which was $150,000 but, it has increased to $300,000. And, the damages of the citizen are not considered since the citizen is only considered to 'be a witness' with the banks and lenders being the victims even though they have insurance against the fraud.

A program established for the foreign nationals as of 2003, to help them 'gain the American Dream' is a program funded for banks to offer reduced rate loans and subsidized loan amounts for illegals who have used other Social Security numbers during their time in America. Only the good credit is transferred to a new Tax Payer ID credit report which is protected by the government, unlike the status of the Social Security Number. With the new report, the subsidized loan is arranged with a lower interest rate. The program is fully documented within *Nation Restoration.*

Father forgive us, for we have loved all who came, helped them and housed them and fed them and trusted that the leadership in the nation were making good decisions. We lacked discernment. We allowed the enemy tactics to unfold within our generations and we repent for ALL that was allowed against the laws of the land for we are to follow the laws and we trusted all 'on the land' would do the same. Forgive us, Father!

The plan which was put into full motion within days of President Woodrow Wilson's inauguration included cooperation from both the House and the Senate!

The plan expanded through the involvement in WWI for an evil purpose but, it was sold to the people to make us think it was good during his second term.

However, truth be told, it was merely an evil world plan which was solidified during the Presidency of Franklin D Roosevelt. Momentum of actions by our government in other nations is exactly what resulted in the attack on us by Japan, resulting in our full global involvement in Europe and in Asia during WWII.

Deeper Truth:

War was NOT over when WWII ended.

It changed from being a war 'over there' to being a war 'here'.

The 'enemy is within our borders' and growing.

That evil plan was fully established with foreign nationals invading our nation 'without documentation' and this status continues 'on our soil' to this day, identical process as *Operation Paperclip.*

The 'operation' is often referred to as the Fourth Reich.

What?

What does that mean?

Fourth Reich only means 'a continuation of the Third Reich'.

Are we really dealing with a structure which merely means a continuation of the Third Reich 'on our soil' as it was exposed under Hitler's leadership in WWII?

YES.

What?

The *Georgia Guidestones* are merely one confirmation of a different plan 'by the other kingdom' which has expanded and is gaining momentum across our nation with the direct links we are 'seeing in plain sight' which connect us to the evil plans of: **The UN, FAKE NEWS, Planned Parenthood and the plan to destroy America.**

The funding and coordination from key sources for *Knights of Pythia, Operation Paperclip and Georgia Guidestones* are identified as being headquartered in Montana!

The funds are extensive.

The key people have purchased the most land in each state in the nation.

Why Did Evil Expand Rapidly After WWII?

Think back to the generation of WWI & WWII' and all of the attributes of that generation: *The Greatest Generation.*

After ALL of the atrocities upon the people, America was still known as the 'blessed nation'. The reason is what made evil plans expand. We declared, as of 1953, that America is ONE NATION UNDER GOD.

At that time families attended church together and Sunday School was 'at the same time' for parents and children. Spouses were 'parents who aligned,' who 'took care of the family, as a family', back when 'mothers were able to be at home, nurturing the next generation', spouses and children were able to prepare and enjoy family meals and relax together during the evenings, without hours of homework required, and spend time 'as a family' during the weekends.

Plus, the income earned was able to 'pay the bills' and companies often built homes for employees to be close to work vs. spending hours commuting to and from work each week.

Family structure, personally, and especially among believers, has shattered from coast to coast due to the changes which are slowly yet consistently aligning us with the evil plan of the world.

Lack of unity at home, in the community and in the government has affected life in America.

Plus, it changed fellowship of the believers because when believers questioned leadership in the church and in the government they were identified as 'disloyal'. Resistance from the leadership to respond 'with the wisdom of the LORD' resulted in believers proceeding without questioning 'to keep the peace'.

This process has been handed down generation to generation for the past 100 years with the youth being instructed to go forth and find out how to be successful in the world and the believers even shifted focus to judge each other which causes division since the 'measuring process' is based upon how successful a person is in the world vs. how far along the person is within the process of being discipled.

When believers care and want to sharpen each other as iron sharpens iron, the person 'being discipled' becomes offended and that status ends the opportunity for 'unity' ... a status which expands as fast as a rushing river!

LIES believed: building credit is a process of building debt!

Families are not able to cover regular bills.

Financial changes destroy ability of families to buy a home.

When a family owns a home and a medical bill or a loss of a job causes them to lose their home, they lose more than the equity!

Families 'on the street' due to a medical issue for a spouse or a child ... forcing the loss of home, savings, vehicles and options.

Are Believers Viewed As Believers Or Worldly People?

Remember when I mentioned how my comments the past 25 years about our nation being a Sodom & Gomorrah due to becoming comfortable so long as me and mine are fine received the response: *It is the End Times ... nobody can change what is happening.*

The sad part of this status is that we stopped 'being the church'. When Christ tabernacled with us, He told us exactly how to proceed 'as the church'.

The church was never a building. We were to become the church for all who have ears to hear and eyes to see. We are to always see to the needs of the widows (without husbands) and orphans (without fathers). So many are 'on the street' and have been there for a long time. When the orphans and foster children are 18, they are 'on their own' whether they know how to proceed in their life or not.

The reason this is critical to our current status in the nation and the church is that the ability to 'overtake' people (traffic children, women) is much easier when the line of authority is not evident!

Important to repent for this status because we have been taken over FROM WITHIN!

The door was opened wide and the enemy entered and became the leadership in our nation without 'documents', i.e., no birth certificates to confirm they were born anywhere, let alone in America. Now, no response to the challenge for production of the documents required to become a candidate for President, documents to confirm being a natural born citizen, is accepted. Why? It is all 'OK' due to the evil plan already accepted in America!

What Did *Operation Paperclip* add to America?

A lot!

It actually operated as a paperclip binding together the global plan and speeding up the globalist, NEW OR ONE WORLD ORDER, ONE WORLD GOVERNMENT AND ALIGNED WITH ONE WORLD RELIGION process while 'leveling the playing field' by eliminating industries, exporting jobs to other nations, draining the economy of the nation by disbursing billions of dollars in 'foreign aid' without accountability while the structure in America resulted in families going bankrupt, losing jobs, homes and experiencing the reduction of the family income.

While citizens are losing, and many are homeless on the streets, even families, the costs for illegals to live in America has become the responsibility of legal citizens.

Now, it is easier to see why the elite have no interest in the citizens WINNING. It was NEVER their plan.

Now we know, we are viewed as 'deplorables' in their sight.

WE WERE NEVER SUPPOSED TO WIN. We were weakened by WWI, even more by WWII, while the government was 'aligned with their evil plans against us' and we did not realize it.

This is why it was a unique moment in time when our Father revealed the 'hold upon us' by *Operation Paperclip.*

I'm not talking about the amazing moment the truth was shared with me, I'm referring to the moments in time when our Father insisted I read the pages out loud!

The pages include so much more than I thought they were going to include.

How did I get through it?

Reading it to the widow, we were shocked ... we took breaks!

It was a time for deeper research for me due to the depth of the layers of deceit *Operation Paperclip* added to everything, to every structure within America, even to our list of Presidents!

Our Father revealed one portion of *Operation Paperclip* to me and another portion of *Operation Paperclip* to Annie Jacobsen. Both sources provided the facts, the historical structure and photos of the people involved in their portion of the huge plan against America.

We were NOT supposed to survive.

Our ability to LIVE and PROSPER is what frustrates them!

The link to the one hour lecture of Annie Jacobsen is provided within the research summary at the end of this book and I highly recommend viewing it when you can arrange some time. Praying it will be a time when you will not be disturbed or distracted.

Her research and documented evidence focuses upon the medical, NASA, research entities, and the many department heads who were not Americans or documented, etc.

The video includes a significant number of photos and facts regarding the specific medical and science 'experts' who entered our nation and became the leaders and entire teams of new, federally funded government departments immediately after WWII.

The location of the current family compound in Kennebunkport, Maine of the George H. Bush family, the 41st President, is the exact location used for the wedding of his father and mother and per the research of Don Nicoloff it was the consistent receiving site for the tens of thousands of undocumented SS agents who entered into America with false stories about their background and in that time in our history it was not easy to research 'false statements' about birth records, etc.

What did they do in America?

They became the people who established the intelligence agencies in America. The research is so deep and specific, it is nearly impossible to summarize.

Therefore, the best option is to set aside some time and review the entire 52 pages of research, photos and documented evidence obtained to confirm the truth. The Idaho Observer article is easy to find in an internet search and the link is provided within the research page at the back of this book.

Both portions, medical / research and the intelligence and government department heads established with people entering our nation during *Operation Paperclip* include many segments of the structure of our nation. It was a massive plan, a huge undertaking with an evil intent, based upon an evil purpose aligned with the 'end game' symbols and the secret societies.

The results of their effort are related directly to the exact issues we are witnessing and dealing with 'in real time' in our nation today. Remember, the agents were also positioned in the media!

At this point in time, we can see the devastation caused within our nation, in our economy, in industry, in medical and scientific endeavors, in our government departments, especially within our intelligence agencies, causing us to be placed in a competition to survive mode in our nation which was a blessed nation of God!

The evil agenda against us has encased us within a web of deceit … a web which is based upon pure evil.

Father forgive us for lacking discernment.

Forgive us for accepting all as good, and often accepting instead of rejecting evil.

Thank you for wrapping Your arms around us NOW, so tight, we will hear Your confirmation of truth even when You whisper so we will ONLY accept all good and reject all evil!

Operation Paperclip resulted in the 41st President being elected without being able to confirm he was natural born! This happened without the public being aware of the truth! It was allowed even though he was a citizen of another nation, serving in the Navy in another nation, Germany, before he served in the Navy in America.

He was able to do all of this 'without documents or legal paperwork' because he was part of a huge invasion into our nation from Europe, specifically Germany.

His 'supposedly adoptive father' was his birth father, also entering our nation and coordinating the plan during WWII from America. His name was not Prescott Bush from birth, the Bush name was the exact name he used, a fake SS name he used in Germany during the war and he used this name 'without documentation' while living in America.

Did you know Prescott Bush became a United States Senator and served in that capacity from 1952 to 1963?

The names, the numbers of people involved, the families controlling many areas of our government, research facilities, etc., the immediate access which allowed them to fill the government departments and proceed with their plans against us, the creation of tax paying departments which did not exist before, the creation and expansion of the intelligence agencies, the infiltrating of other nations, changing their leadership while supposedly 'representing America', removing patriots from our agencies in America and damaging their lives for the rest of their time 'on earth'.

Now, is a moment to take a breath. I was prompted to summarize it in a way to help 'grasp the magnitude' of the evil

If you stopped and took a breath, please re-read it.

It was an invasion which took place with ease because they did not come in through a port or an airport, or 'sign in' at Ellis Island as legal immigrants did prior to this 'change in HIStory'.

Many have tried to stand up against this invasion, against the lawlessness, to bring truth to the people and yet, they have been removed, often due to loss of their own life.

Father forgive us!

Operation Paperclip was researched by an investigative reporter for the Idaho Observer in April 2007, after a man heard the truth from the same source due to dating the daughter of the source.

Who was the source? Otto Skorzeny.

He chose to share the facts, photographs and business details with his potential son-in-law. Eric 'Orion' Berman. Skorzeny also shared the facts during a Republic Broadcasting Network radio interview January 17, 2006.

Who was the investigative reporter? Don Nicoloff.

The article is easily accessible. It includes photographs and specifics to confirm the summary provided by Nicoloff when he released the first installment of his series of articles in the Idaho Observer in April 2007. Beginning of the introductory statement to the first installment of his series of articles: *What you are about to read is another step beyond research pioneered in the early 90s by author/historian Webster Tarpley based largely on deathbed "clues" provided by former Hitler bodyguard Otto Skorzeny and his box of photographs. Since Skorzeny's death in 1999, the*

134

various leads he provided have been followed up and tend to support what, at first blush, would appear to be the unbelievable rantings of an embittered old man.

The article includes photos and extensive, documented research which proves a different story about the Bush and Walker families.

The truth is revealed.

The truth is tough to view 'in print'.

However, the depth of research into the family proves the facts we did not know & confirms the stories we were told, were lies.

Facts which prove the lies were accepted as truth and the lies allowed a rise to power which would not be possible if we were aligned as believers operating in discernment. The facts provided within these articles help us connect the dots so we can finally realize 'how we got here'.

What has unfolded in the past few years is 'not a new plan', it is a repeated phase of the 'master plan' aligned with the enemy's plan against believers.

We are clearly expendable.

We were not important within any phase of the enemy's plan.

The terms we are hearing from the people aligned with the enemy's plan attempt to discredit us, our voice and our purpose and plan 'while on earth'.

Deplorables, a polite way of evil plotters to describe believers!

What did the reporter find?

Birth and school documented evidence does not exist to support or align with the stories stated as facts by the Bush family.

Even Otto Skorzeny thought the adoption story was real while he actually knew the life in Germany and America of the 41st President & his birth father, yet Prescott Bush was 'in America'.

Research facts clearly prove the truth and provide the truth. The article is 52 pages if you cut and paste the article installments, including the photos, into a WORD document.

Is there more evil than this in the plan? YES.

When you review the information within the article about the evil plan and actions taken against the inventor, Tesla, you will be shocked to your very core!

Prior to reviewing the article, our Father sat with me while I viewed a 'biography marathon' (or so it seemed) of the 'money people': Rockefeller, Carnegie, J P Morgan and Getty. It would NOT be something I would have been interested in, not even one-percent! However, our Father wanted me to hear specifics!

Tesla. Did you know IF Tesla's inventions would have been funded by people who were FOR AMERICA instead of being people who were NOT interested in the nation, only in the padding of their personal pockets until they were overflowing with cash, we would never pay for electricity?

There would not be a need for power lines or utility bills for electricity!

Tesla was brought to America, used and destroyed by the money people 'in power positions' controlling business and government back at that time!

Skorzeny knew the truth and provided the whole truth.

The money deals that the money men (family dynasty men) proceeded upon were directed toward 'win at any cost'.

The battles 'between them' resulted in a different outcome in many areas of inventions, inventors, industries and how we do business in our nation. Men who were clearly established within the global elite as dynasty structures; names 'in charge' to this day.

Saving some really great facts about Tesla for the last Chapter, when we have a moment to digest the horrible, criminal actions taken against Tesla, in business and in life, financially, mentally and in the entire destruction of one of the most, if not the very top name on the list of prolific inventors in all of history.

Realizing what he was made aware of ... what he accomplished ... what was being made available for our world ... Tesla had to be aligned with a GOD plan!

California. Sharing as an example since many think and declare 'no Christians standing up in California – because, if they would, things would be different'.

Did you know that the Getty family has controlled California for more than 80 years?

Names of the leadership 'in control' the past decades:

Brown (father & son, as governor, etc.),

Newsome (prior generations and current governor), with family 'obtaining Squaw Valley after the Olympics' from their relative, the Governor at the time, and even

Pelosi ... limb upon limb ... They are all related to each other generation upon generation, and each family fills a limb of the Getty family tree.

In 2019, California was still not able to certify many of the elections since they were still proceeding with a plan to invite voters to 'be on a jury'. Per the Assemblyman, 500,000 + in San Diego County alone responded 'Not a citizen'. Many did not respond. Warrant for their arrest is not know ... not reported.

Trusting you are amazed with the facts being revealed about the depth of the plan put in place and carried out 'on the land' and then, around the globe, a web of deceit which expanded beyond comprehension. It's a tough pill to swallow when we realize it has ALL, in America and other nations, been funded by legal tax paying citizens in our nation.

Father forgive us!

We desire to hear Your voice, walk in faith with clarity based upon hearing Your truth, wisdom with discernment granted to us when we invite You into each situation.

We will not allow the enemy to continue to operate within a 'master plan' against believers!

We stand firm aligned with you as believers, uniting together while we pray to You, our Father, Hallowed be Your Name, Your Kingdom come, Your will be done for we realize now that You sent us to earth for these specific days in HIStory to help it become on earth as it is in heaven.

We praise You and thank You for being our rear-guard and for loving us through our many training phases as we learn to stand so firm before we put on the armor that we can stand against any powers and principalities for You are with us in the midst of the battle and victory is ours before the battle even begins. Grateful for the opportunity to serve! AMEN

Chapter 5   Monarch Mentality

The world kingdom operates within the monarchy structure, enslaving the people to 'follow the commands, the decisions, the opinions of those in positions of POWER over the people'.

America was formed as a nation where the people decide, citizens choose to proceed per the laws established and based upon the bible. Therefore, because we allowed actions with evil intent to proceed and the ten commandments to be removed from our courts, we are now directly affected by those who operate with an evil intent.

How did this happen?

We trusted and when we granted our trust to the untrustworthy, we actually formed an alliance, a pact with those who operate within an evil agenda.

The worldly 'monarchy' kingdom structure requires: control, power, greed, for the domination over everything in the kingdom, the nation, the land, and all of the possessions, especially including ALL of the people!

Then, the other kingdom has only one question: *Will you bow?*

If you believe Israel was a blessed nation and life was always great for the people and that is why many hope to return to 'the land', you may want to do a little research into 'who controlled' the nation of Israel!

None of the 19 kings were men of GOD in the North where the famous 'ten lost tribes' resided until they were taken captive by Assyria. Southern portion of the land, Judah, including the remaining two tribes, Judah and Benjamin, occasionally had a king who knew GOD and honored GOD so he would reform the government. However, the people were eventually marched off to Babylon!

We have a choice to make!

To reveal how quickly life can change based upon a change in leadership of a monarchy, we merely need to review **II Chronicles** to see what happens when there is a change in leadership or in the alliance(s) of the leader.

In the beginning of Chapter 20, Jehoshaphat (his name means judged by GOD, a man in the direct lineage of King David) who declared and decreed who the LORD is and how the people will stand firm with the LORD.

Then, how life changed quickly due to making a personal plan by aligning with a worldly king at the end of the same chapter.

There is a greater change in the region within the next chapter, **II Chronicles 21,** a change which was not good.

When Jehoram, the son of Jehoshaphat, became king after his death, he immediately changed the focus 180 degrees!

His father strengthened the people, the nation but, Jehoram (849 to 842 BC) chose to strengthen himself by killing all of his brothers with the sword, and the princes of Israel.

He eliminated all potential competition to his rule.

Did he have an outside influence?

He was married to Athaliah (his consort).

Who was she?

Daughter of Ahab and Jezebel.

Who reigned after Jehoram died?

Son of Jehoram and Athaliah, Ahaziah.

Did he return to the kingdom to the LORD? **NO!**

Athaliah influenced Jehoram and Ahaziah due to Baal worship.

How long was the reign of Ahaziah? **One Year.**

He was murdered due to a pre-planned coup.

***Who reigned after the death of Ahaziah?* His mother.**

Athaliah became queen consort due to her standing.

Later, her title changed to Queen Regnant (dominate reign).

***How long did she reign?* 841 BC to 835 BC.**

It matters who 'reigns in the world' while it absolutely matters much more to us and our lineage when we know that we know who reigns 'over our life'!

Our LORD is the same yesterday, today and tomorrow!

The scriptures confirm what we face DOES NOT CHANGE, it is the same evil plan from the beginning!

WE ARE THE ONES WHO AFFECT THE OUTCOME.

Who do you serve?

Who does your family serve?

We are at a critical time to NOT be on the fence, to absolutely make our choice.

Feel free to do a little historical research.

Republic of America

When our nation was formed, it was formed as a Republic where We The People were the voice in the land. The government is US. We form it, we say how it proceeds and we proceed per the laws of the bible, the ten commandments.

Why were the ten commandments taken out of courts?

Why were crosses removed from battle fields?

We forgot it is OUR government.

We stopped being the voice!

We became a silent majority!

We let the enemy enter in and rule on the land.

We allowed the plans of the enemy to become the way it is around here!

What we were thinking?

Were we thinking while living our life upon the blessed land?

What has happened is a direct repeat!

The people of God were enslaved in Egypt.

Freed and yet, returned to being 'enslaved' to idols.

Many perished and did NOT enter into the promised land.

Then, our Father re-named Jacob. His new name was Israel.

Israel, formerly the family of Jacob, consisted of twelve sons.

Each son became a tribe, a family clan of the name of each son.

How did ten tribes become 'the ten lost tribes of Israel'?

They were in the North of Israel. They had nineteen kings and each king was evil. The people were taken captive by Assyria.

What happened to the two tribes in the South, Judah and Benjamin, with the region known as Judah? Occasionally they had a king who followed God and the king reformed the kingdom during his reign.

However, the kingdom was also ruled by evil kings and the region of Judah did not remain free. The people were marched off to Babylon.

God gave the people of Israel a second chance. He arranged for them to journey to the uninhabited regions of the world, to establish themselves with the guidance of our Father.

Did they? Some did.

Some truly passed on the truth generation to generation from the elders to the youth, so the truth would be known in future generations.

In the prior books, I shared a few facts received from the chiefs of the tribes and the truth is evident in their review of HIStory.

Their devotion to our Father and desire to follow Him no matter the circumstances is clearly evident within their personal testimonies. Truth resonates the moment it is heard and the words remain in the heart and mind forever!

This was the desire of our Father.

He sent us to help it become on earth as it is in heaven.

However, in whatever form you see the body of believers living in during the current day status, leaving the future up to the leadership is evident in the speaking within the church as much as it is within the world.

Whether we say – God will take care of it – God will position the right people to change it – we are actually blaming God for how it will turn out. When it does not turn the way we hoped, we go into hope deferred. We do not promote men and women of God for the positions in leadership in our community, our states or our nation. As men and women of God, we are to be in the positions of leadership and accountable to the people, the nation for upholding biblical principles.

However, during the decades of my life (while the number of decades is clearly not important), I've always been told to leave the politics to politicians and not discuss politics or religion with anyone. Therefore, due to taking this stand within the body of believers, we have left the entire government structure open to the enemy and we have not shared our faith with people in our region. **Bottom line:** Nobody was holding the politicians or the leaders in the body of believers accountable. Life was not getting better. No matter who was in the position, the status did not change.

By stating God will fix it, God will take care of it, God will position the people in government as the body of believers, we were actually saying we are not accountable for anything while we are here. Therefore, we allowed all of the destruction, fraud and corruption to happen during our shift!

By separating ourselves from government and leadership, we became the slaves of those in power.

We did not discern the truth.

We trusted. We did not see that their intent was evil.

We did not realize they desired to change everything from divine law to their laws and their style of justice until we became the victims to their lawlessness and injustices.

So much has been revealed and yet, many in our nation are still unaware of the depth of evil planned against us.

Separation of Church and State

We are not alone in our 'occasional alignment with the other kingdom'.

We are not the first generation to surrender vs. stand firm.

The Founding Fathers knew the challenge!

The formation of the Constitution and Declaration of Independence were critical in the wording to keep the power and authority with the people, not the leadership; people governance.

The protection was established to not allow the leader of the nation to become the leader of the church.

However, what happened over time?

The government took over the entire structure of leadership, including the church, across the nation. Government reporting and restrictions were put in place to control the gathering of believers 'as a church'.

The state still took over the church even though we are not established as a monarchy.

We aligned so much, we hear people constantly state they want the leadership to 'fix it' – God put the leadership 'in position' – and, in their position, they are to 'fix it' so it aligns with God's plan.

If We The People are not aligned with God's plan, how can the leadership represent us based upon God's plan, and proceed with us according to God's plan?

We have work to do!

Father forgive us for blaming leaders, and especially for blaming You for how things are turning out. Forgive us for we have neglected to seek Your truth, Your purpose and plan for our life while we are on earth endeavoring to make it become on earth as it is in heaven. Forgive us for NOT turning from our wicked ways so we can hear Your voice and proceed upon Your plan and help others in our region align with You as our territory expands so leadership in our region, our state and our nation realize Your truth, Your purpose and plan for us in these days so we will be aligned, united so it shall become on earth as it is in heaven. Praying we are becoming Your remnant for our desire is to serve You, for me and my house ONLY serving You, Father!

Father knew the world was filled with evil and chaos.

Often, very often, I receive an identical request. *Why would God send us to a world filled with evil & chaos?*

He trusts us!

He knew the plans He had for us, before the earth was formed!

He knew He could send us NOW, when fraud and corruption had already permeated the governing process for decades and yet, it was not revealed in news stories on a daily basis until these days.

He loved the world so much, He sent His son who paved the way and paid the price for our Father to send us, joint-heirs to proceed without hesitation because we are fully protected by the blood!

149

This is why Christ taught us to pray for life to become on earth as it is in heaven. We are given full power and authority to proceed.

Since I do not want to attempt to persuade you to participate fully by hearing only a phrase. Let's review the process so we can stand firm in the days ahead, getting into position as We The People who will proceed and live in truth:

Our Father

Who Art In Heaven

HALLOWED BE THY NAME

THY KINGDOM COME

THY WILL BE DONE

ON EARTH AS IT IS IN HEAVEN

Give us This Day our Daily Bread

And Forgive us our (Debts) Trespasses

As we forgive (Debtors) those who Trespass against us

And lead us not into temptation

Deliver us from evil

For Thine is the Kingdom, and the power, and the glory, forever and ever. AMEN

Remember the Tower of Babel?

Well, there are 72 chiefs/tribes of Babel, 60 more than Israel!

They are very active, especially in lending and industry to this day. The 'other kingdom' is in all aspects of life on earth!

Much to pray about! When we throw up our hands and we forget or choose to not seek our purpose and plan for being on earth in these days, we are giving up even though we do not think of it as surrendering to the enemy, it is exactly what we are doing.

WE ARE TO POSSESS THE LAND
UNTIL CHRIST RETURNS.

ANOTHER ROOT: Another plan to 'control the people'.

A religion was formed, linked to Aeons.

While being prompted to 'listen to the news' in the last few days, I heard a US Congressman quote Aleister Crowley.

Over time, I have heard the name but, I have not researched the name.

Immediately after hearing the quote, I was prompted to do some research: Another link to the 'other kingdom', like Rathbone, Pike and Bailey. Same evil plan, just a new structure developed to reach the same goal:

1. Aleister Crowley formed a religion: **Thelema.**

2. Became a self-proclaimed prophet.

3. Declared: Entrusted to lead humanity into Aeon of Horus.

4. Published his writings as *Oracles* and *The Book of the Law.*

5. Studied Hindu, Buddhism, Islamic mysticism and Arabic.

6. An occultist, satanist, believing in a Father God.

7. Believed last three Aeons are:

    1. Aeon of Isis,

2. Aeon of Osiris,

3. Aeon of Horus in 1904, focused upon self-realization and self-actualization, with the belief of becoming God-Men, witnessing the resurrection of the sun god, Ra.

Crowley declared he joined the Masons while in Mexico. Isis and Osiris are two of the gods within the oaths. The two are mentioned within *A Wake Up Call: It's Restoration Time* while the facts about the main 'sun god' celebrated on December 25 (there were many who were declared to be sun gods; ALL are dead) are provided and the specifics confirm the Satanic counterfeit within my book on *Christmas.*

Insert from my *Christmas* book: Isis and Osiris.

Mithra, known as the unconquered sun god / son.

Who was Mithra?

Some sources confirm he was the son of **Osiris** the Egyptian king of the dead, and **Isis** (sister of Osiris; children of Nut; births resulted in the curse of Re being removed; they married since a god can only marry a goddess; Isis insisted she channeled the secret of Ra and passed it on to Osiris and to Mithra to retain the power; Ra was a sun god in the 24th and 25th centuries BC) an Egyptian goddess of magic, fertility, and motherhood.

How was Mithra referred to by the followers?

The lamb.

In fact, he was often depicted in drawings with a lamb being carried on his shoulders.

He was honored as the son of god and the good shepherd.

Plus, followers trusted Mithra was the way, the truth, the light, the life, and the word.

Celebrations were made similar for both the pagans and Christians: baptisms, communion and Sunday worship which was established as the 'day of rest to honor the sun god' by Constantine.

Followers of Mithra were considered as a cult. Including goddess worship of his mother resulted in the title: Cult of Isis.

The teachings through this 'religion' Crowley created have become quite popular and many published articles confirm their plan is declared 'in print'. Their plan is focused upon replacing the Christian God. The information is easy to find within any search regarding the Aeon of Horus.

What is the main focus: POWER, control over the people.

The religion celebrates many of the Satanic dates, including the special days for their worship during solstice.

The internet photos of the Aeon of Horus wanted a fee for copyright and I do not want to insert the image that bad.

Within moments, while I was taking a break after this unique time of research, our Father prompted me to look at something which seemed silly: *Photos: Houses owned by news media, entertainers ...each one worth millions.*

Since I was not interested in viewing photos of mansions, I clicked on a few and then I decided to exit. Before I clicked, our Father prompted me to NOT exit, yet. After clicking on a couple more photos, the next headline confirmed a well known model received a gift of the most expensive home in the world, a 390 million dollar home in Turkey. The model is Naomi Campbell.

When I clicked to see the picture, the home and property revealed the exact design of the Aeon (eye) of Horus.

Remember the oracle in Greece?

Because Apollo was 'in charge' – his daughter, Pythia, was considered the top oracle or counsel in the world at that time. The people traveled great distances, by foot, to hear the messages from the Oracle on the 7th day of the month.

Aleister Crowley structured a very similar plan, purpose and type or worship to *The Aeon of Horus.*

Thinking about what has happened to us as legal residents on the land, and the lack of discernment displayed in throwing up our hands and trusting leadership will take care of it … we actually became aligned with the other kingdom and allowed ourselves and our families to align with the plans of the world.

This is how the world enslaves the people.

This is why repentance, daily, the moment we realize we have drifted (slightly or more than slightly) away from the plan for our life for this day, is critical for us and for our families.

Imagine what life would have been like, before Christ.

People believed in God.

People sought God's truth.

People aligned with the believers when they heard truth.

Believers throughout the region gathered to fellowship.

500 – 600 BC, Tribes of Israel were in various parts of the uninhabited lands long before, in fact, a few centuries before Christ.

Did they all remain aligned with God? No.

Did they all align with Christ? No.

The question has not changed over the centuries: *Who does your family, your house, serve?*

More aligned with God in early times and with Christ than with Noah, while the truth is Noah was fully aligned with God!

Noah was the only pastor during his century of effort, cutting the lumber and building the ark.

Noah's days of sharing God's truth with all in the region were extended for more than 100 years. He shared the truth with all who would listen and with all who questioned the fact he was building an ark when the 'rain' always came up from the earth and not 'falling from the sky'.

Noah shared the same truth each and every day,.

Truth was the same the entire time he was building the ark.

Who believed Noah? Nobody!

Not one person chose to believe the truth or enter the ark.

How committed are we to sharing the truth God reveals to us?

It was three years 'boots on ground in Georgia' when I passionately confirmed to God that it was absolutely time for me to receive a new assignment.

That's right, I knew that I knew it was time for me to go elsewhere!

Why?

The people were not listening, they were not willing to unite together as believers to become a voice, to stand firm proclaiming the truth in these days.

Evidence 'in hand' proved this fact!

When the Graham Cooke message 'unite within five to ten years' was shared with me as a confirmation of the word our Father asked me to share with the leadership, it was disheartening to find out the message was delivered to the same leadership 22 years prior to my days in Georgia, Twenty-two years!

A shock to realize I used the exact words God clearly gave to Graham Cooke to send him from England to Macon, Georgia (not New York or Chicago or Los Angeles or Dallas) the first time our Father sent him on an assignment to America, and I added intensity which appeared to be expressed more like a battering ram or an AK-47 (sounds bold, especially since I have difficulty with a 357 magnum!), completely forgetting in this moment that it was God who also sent me to Macon, Georgia (not NY or LA ...). God knew the leadership before He sent Graham Cooke, and He knew they would be the same leadership operating in the same ministries and same manner the entire 22 years until he sent me.

Plus, God knew I would become frustrated because He knows I want to see results!

He absolutely knows the end from the beginning!

Remember the story about the mouse to the elephant? The powerful man of God told me he saw a vision and he was satisfied to bite on the ankle of the elephant but, I would not stop. I ran up and swung on the tail, screaming for the elephant to MOVE! Then, I bit on the ear and screamed. Then, on the other ear and screamed until the elephant moved. He said it was tearful for him when our Father confirmed the elephant represented the body of Christ and therefore, he was OK with the status and he stopped where he was.

See? Even I forget the truth when I am 'in the questioning mode' of WHY ME – WHY HERE – WHY NOW?

God Uses Other People When We Need To Hear Truth

The very next day, I was at a bible study. The leader said she was going to share something for someone's benefit, a topic which was not going to be part of the bible study. I was sitting in the front row, ready for the special message for someone!

As soon as she shared the Noah facts and confirmed Noah did not surrender, quit ... God had 100% of my attention and repentance ... wow, she was clearly talking directly to me, giving me a message direct from our Father.

While she shared the truth about the 100+ years of Noah, I was in deep repentance. After I was done, our Father reminded me that I am here, exactly as we are all here, to seed the lives of the people in our daily path with God's truth!

And, again, as our Father confirmed to me, if it takes 1000 messengers to touch the heart of the person, it does not matter if we are number 575 or 999, we may not see the results. However, the fact we touched the heart of the person, that is what matters to our Father!

Yikes.

A hard pill to swallow at times, while it is the truth! The soul is what is important to the Father and impacting the life as a true representative so all may become well with their soul is the goal!

Will we keep sharing the truth no matter what?

Will we keep the truth to ourselves when others do not want to listen?

Or, will we stop speaking the truth and align with the world?

When we stop, we surrender.

When we surrender, we align with the other kingdom.

It is not new to stand for truth, become discouraged when nobody listens to the truth and think our effort is for naught.

Father knows our heart and Christ resides in our heart!

Father we thank You for not giving up on us, for not forsaking us and for continuing to train us as we walk forward in faith for we do realize this is an evil world and yet, we are honored to know You trust us and we can come to You for the truth each day for You know the plans you have for us and we stand firm with You for You know the end from the beginning and You have only good laid out before us so we will do all we can to share the truth and help set the captives free. Father we are grateful You chose to send us to the world now, with a purpose and plan You just for us so we can unite together with fellow believers and realize how we an align with You to help it become on earth as it is in heaven. Thank you Father!

Chapter 6   God's Master Plan Trumps Enemy's Master Plan

Before the earth was formed and the seas and land 'positioned' … before it all, we were part of our Father's plan!

The scripture 'about us' is so powerful. Paul's description to the believers in Ephesus, especially when I think about the spiritual battle they conquered and the stand they took after being part of the world and all who worshiped Diana across Europe. The Temple of Diana was formerly the Temple of Artemis, the twin of Apollo, daughter of Zeus and Leto, the Aunt of the Delphi Oracle, Pythia.

Oracle of Delphi

Delphi, where people gathered to worship the Oracle, Pythia, in the Temple of Artemis and then, it became the Temple of Diana.

Temple of Diana of Ephesus.

Paul's description of who we are is so clear in Ephesians, I am so blessed each time I read it, I could insert the entire chapter!

The depth of who we are is significant.

Why? We are here, in this nation, in the midst of Pythian castles and secret society plans.

Regardless of our circumstances, the situations we may find ourselves in today are no different than ancient times. We are at a time of choosing: *Who will we serve?*

We have the same opportunity every day to speak the TRUTH to the people in the world.

Some may have taken an oath but, they can renounce it! Some may be deeply involved in a secret society but, they can renounce it! Some may be affected by or caught up in the worship of an idol or an entity, whether the worship is by people who may be naive or innocent, or the rituals have have taken on meaning to them over time but, they can renounce it!

GOD gives us second chances!

We can REPENT and be RESTORED to who HE sent to earth so it will become on earth 'as it is in heaven'!

Our goal is to proclaim the truth, no matter what with emphasis on the 'no matter what'!

Remember, when Paul was stoned and was left for dead out side the city wall, our Father raised him up and transported him to another city to preach! Our Father loves each of us as much as He loved Paul!

The LORD over ALL does not love any one of us one ounce more than any other one of us!

In fact, HE asked me when I said I was being persecuted, spoken against, *Did they stone you* (me) *to death?* A speechless pause happened – felt like a HOLY HUSH – and, I had to be honest when I responded, *Of course they did not but, it was really, really bad.*

Without hesitation our Father said, *If they stoned you* (me) *to death I would raise you* (me) *up and transport you* (me) *to another city to preach.*

Without realizing the fact I was evidently looking for a little more compassion, some sympathy due to the situation and how I felt (I should have remembered, feelings LIE – however, I was forgetting that fact in this moment), so I continued on the same path: *Last week they really loved me but, this week I am hearing a different story* (clearly, more self-pity requesting comments!) ... Again, without hesitation, our Father asked, *Are they cutting down a tree and forming it into a cross?* This time, I was alert and quicker on the draw with my response, *Of course they are not but, it's such a change from last week* ...(clearly, a few more pity requesting comments!) Again, our Father provided clear direction without hesitation, *Well then, you are doing good and you can go forward and preach.*

The journey of Paul has been a precious lesson which I am still learning with each phase of each new assignment! God is faithful!

Paul preaching to the people in Ephesus:

Ephesians 1:3-14. *Blessed be the God and Father of our Lord Jesus Christ, who has blessed us with every spiritual blessing in the heavenly places in Christ, 4 just as He chose us in Him before the foundation of the world, that we should be holy and without blame before Him in love, 5 having predestined us to adoption as sons by Jesus Christ to Himself, according to the good pleasure of His will, 6 to the praise of the glory of His grace, by which He made us accepted in the Beloved.*

7 In Him we have redemption through His blood, the forgiveness of sins, according to the riches of His grace 8 which He made to abound toward us in all wisdom and prudence, 9 having made known to us the mystery of His will, according to His good pleasure which He purposed in Himself, 10 that in the dispensation of the fullness of the times He might gather together in one, all things in Christ, both which are in heaven and which are on earth—in Him. 11 In Him also we have obtained an inheritance, being predestined according to the purpose of Him who works all things according to the counsel of His will, 12 that we who first trusted in Christ should be to the praise of His glory.

13 In Him you also trusted, after you heard the word of truth, the gospel of your salvation; in whom also, having believed, you were sealed with the Holy Spirit of promise, 14 who is the guarantee of our inheritance until the redemption of the purchased possession, to the praise of His glory.

What is the glory?

Uniting with the Father 'in HIS presence', receiving HIS truth.

John 17:22, within John 17:9-26. (Christ confirmed to our Father) *"I pray for them. I do not pray for the world but for those whom You have given Me, for they are Yours. 10 And all Mine are Yours, and Yours are Mine, and I am glorified in them.*

11 *Now I am no longer in the world, but these are in the world, and I come to You. Holy Father, keep through Your name those whom You have given Me, that they may be one as We are.* 12 *While I was with them in the world, I kept them in Your name. Those whom You gave Me I have kept; and* <u>*none of them is lost except the son of perdition*</u>*, that the Scripture might be fulfilled.* 13 *But now I come to You, and these things I speak in the world, that they may have My joy fulfilled in themselves.* 14 *I have given them Your word; and the world has hated them because they are not of the world, just as I am not of the world.* 15 *I do not pray that You should take them out of the world, but that You should keep them from the evil one.* 16 *They are not of the world, just as I am not of the world.* 17 *Sanctify them by Your truth. Your word is truth.* 18 *As You sent Me into the world, I also have sent them into the world.* 19 *And for their sakes I sanctify Myself, that they also may be sanctified by the truth.*

20 *"I do not pray for these alone, but also for those who will believe in Me through their word;* 21 *that they all may be one, as You, Father, are in Me, and I in You; that they also may be one in Us, that the world may believe that You sent Me.* 22 *And the glory which You gave Me I have given them, that they may be one just as We are one:* 23 *I in them, and You in Me; that they may be made perfect in one, and that the world may know that You have sent Me, and have loved them as You have loved Me.*

24 *"Father, I desire that they also whom You gave Me may be with Me where I am, that they may behold My glory which You*

have given Me; for You loved Me before the foundation of the world. 25 O righteous Father! The world has not known You, but I have known You; and these have known that You sent Me. 26 And I have declared to them Your name, and will declare it, that the love with which You loved Me may be in them, and I in them."

We are victorious!

Everything was prepared for us!

Father has never left us or forsaken us!

Christ came, prepared the path, for HE is the WAY for us!

Everything was done for us!

We became joint-heirs with Christ, with all power & authority!

Everything was given to us!

Christ TOOK THE KEYS from the enemy!

The enemy has NO POWER over us!

The enemy has to share lies to place us in fear, doubt and unbelief so he can steal, kill and destroy 'in our mind' the plans our Father has laid out before us, plans our FATHER purposed for us before the foundation of the earth!

Remember the declaration and decree of King Jehoshaphat?

What was the result?

II Chronicles 20: 13-30.

Now all Judah, with their little ones, their wives, and their children, stood before the LORD.

14 Then the Spirit of the LORD came upon Jahaziel the son of Zechariah, the son of Benaiah, the son of Jeiel, the son of Mattaniah, a Levite of the sons of Asaph, in the midst of the assembly.

NOTE: After five generations: Jahaziel.

From the beginning of our nation, five generations, then US!

LORD speak YOUR truth through US!

Our desire is to gather ALL believers together and stand firm, aligned with YOU against the evil in this nation and around the world!

15 And he said, *"Listen, all you of Judah and you inhabitants of Jerusalem, and you, King Jehoshaphat! Thus says the LORD to you: 'Do not be afraid nor dismayed because of this great multitude, for the battle is not yours, but God's. 16 Tomorrow go down against them. They will surely come up by the Ascent of Ziz, and you will find them at the end of the brook before the Wilderness of Jeruel. 17 You will not need to fight in this battle. Position yourselves, stand still and see the salvation of the LORD, who is with you, O Judah and Jerusalem!' Do not fear or be dismayed; tomorrow go out against them, for the LORD is with you."*

18 And Jehoshaphat bowed his head with *his* face to the ground, and all Judah and the inhabitants of Jerusalem bowed before the LORD, worshiping the LORD. **19** Then the Levites of the children of the Kohathites and of the children of the Korahites stood up to praise the LORD God of Israel with voices loud and high.

20 So they rose early in the morning and went out into the Wilderness of Tekoa; and as they went out, Jehoshaphat stood and said, *"Hear me, O Judah and you inhabitants of Jerusalem: Believe in the Lord your God, and you shall be established; believe His prophets, and you shall prosper."* **21** *And when he had consulted with the people, he appointed those who should sing to the Lord, and who should praise the beauty of holiness, as they went out before the army and were saying:*

"Praise the Lord,

For His mercy endures forever."

22 Now when they began to sing and to praise, the Lord set ambushes against the people of Ammon, Moab, and Mount Seir, who had come against Judah; and they were defeated. **23** For the people of Ammon and Moab stood up against the inhabitants of Mount Seir to utterly kill and destroy them. And when they had made an end of the inhabitants of Seir, they helped to destroy one another.

24 So when Judah came to a place overlooking the wilderness, they looked toward the multitude; and there were their dead bodies, fallen on the earth. No one had escaped.

25 When Jehoshaphat and his people came to take away their spoil, they found among them an abundance of valuables on the dead bodies, and precious jewelry, which they stripped off for themselves, more than they could carry away; and they were three days gathering the spoil because there was so much. **26** And on the fourth day they assembled in the Valley of Berachah, for there they blessed the Lord; therefore the name of that place was called The Valley of Berachah until this day. **27** Then they returned, every man of Judah and Jerusalem, with Jehoshaphat in front of them, to go back to Jerusalem with joy, for the Lord had made them rejoice over their enemies. **28** So they came to Jerusalem, with stringed instruments and harps and trumpets, to the house of the Lord. **29** And the fear of God was on all the kingdoms of those countries when they heard that the Lord had fought against the enemies of Israel. **30** Then the realm of Jehoshaphat was quiet, for his God gave him rest all around. (Underlining, added)

Our Father's 'Master Plan' is laid out in His word!

HIS plans are for us to prosper, to live an abundant life!

We are here to DEMONSTRATE as Christ did 'while on earth'.

SAME PLAN: For it to become on earth as it is in heaven!

HE planned for Christ to come to earth to demonstrate LIFE to us, not to present through a lecture how we could find the WAY. Christ LIVED as a surrendered believer to ONLY do what the

LORD does, SAY what the LORD says, a demonstration for us by BEING the WAY, the WORD, the TRUTH while in human form!

No matter how much the world has affected any of the believers during their time on earth, the nation named America still became a blessed nation of God, as ONE NATION UNDER GOD, with the people gathering 'on the land' who knew the truth and were willing to sacrifice everything, so the nation could be formed per the WORD OF THE ONLY LIVING LORD!

We are already victorious!

We have already won the battle.

We are victorious WHERE WE PLACE OUR FEET.

The enemy is a liar and has no option left within his plan.

We were to become as wise as the serpent so we would understand he LIES … all he has are LIES … he LOST! Christ holds the keys and ONLY the FATHER knows the 'MASTER PLAN'! The enemy is unaware and NOT included!

We have ALL of the promises and ALL of the power and authority to align with our Father while the powers and principalities are dealt with … the captives are set free … all we have to do is stop allowing divisions among the true believers and unite together as joint-heirs during our time on earth, re-aligned to the TRUTH to proceed upon our Father's plan for it to become on earth as it is in heaven.

There are glorious days planned for us!

The lies of the enemy are being revealed and we are confirmed as the CONQUERORS.

The evil rituals of the other kingdom are being brought out into the light and exposed to all who have ears to hear and eyes to see.

More people are seeking the truth and the Holy Spirit to know the voice of our Father than ever before.

Christ is appearing before people of faith AND of other faiths and revealing our Father's truth directly to them. The people are standing in awe as they share their testimonies far and wide!

Testimony shared by Pastor Rodney Howard-Browne.

Insert from *For The Sake Of America II:*

Deeply grateful for the truth shared each time I've heard Rodney in San Diego from the 1990's forward; in October 2015 in Thomasville, Georgia, witnessing evidence the people are waking up to the truth, and in June 2016 in Columbus, Georgia where Rodney shared an amazing testimony of another Daniel.

Daniel was attending seminary. He felt he needed to leave so he could do what GOD wanted him to do, say what GOD wanted him to say and go where GOD wanted him to go.

He wanted Rodney's counsel. His decision was already clear!

Immediately after Daniel left the seminary, the LORD asked him to buy a new bible and travel to Yemen.

Daniel was shocked GOD would send him to a Muslim country.

GOD merely reminded Daniel what he said he wanted to do because now, GOD was asking him to go.

Daniel bought the new bible, packed and flew to Yemen.

After he was settled in at the hotel, he prayed.

GOD merely gave him the address where the bible was to be delivered the next morning.

Daniel was shocked.

The address was in the Muslim section of Yemen!

GOD merely reminded Daniel of his request, his desire to go where GOD needed him to go. Daniel confirmed he would deliver the bible in the morning.

When Daniel arrived, he was a bit nervous while knocking on the door. A man answered and opened the door wide. The home was filled with people dressed in Muslim attire.

Daniel handed the bible to the man who was crying while he accepted the bible and said, *Thank you Daniel.*

Daniel was shocked the man knew his name. When he asked the man how he knew his name, the man said, *Jesus visited our home last night. He said He was sending His representative Daniel to bring us a bible so we can read it and know the truth.*

PLAGUES

We are witnessing the plagues around the globe in these days!

LOCUSTS – 2019. Mecca. So many. Layers of dead locusts inside the mosque in Mecca. Then, **Locusts in Yemen:**

Rivers Turn to Blood 'Over Night'

BLOOD RED RIVERS – appearing 'over night'.

February 2018:   A river in Lebanon.

July 2018:   A river in China.

January 2019:   Linthipe River in Dedza, Africa.

September 2019: Daldykan River, located above Arctic Circle!

Plus, reports from America, Australia, Sri Lanka, the Netherlands, in addition to the above.

These Are The Days

The truth is the truth!

There are NO VERSIONS of the truth!

The people are drawing close to the Father, more so due to seeking truth in these days than at any time in HIStory!

Father we are deeply grateful You loved us so much You sent your SON. Then, You sent us to this earth for these exact days because You love us so much and You knew us so well that You sent us as the answer to the cries of the people in the world. You knew they would need each of us in these unique days! Thank you for loving us so much and trusting us so much! AMEN

Chapter 7   God's Trump Card

Not easy to withhold the truth about God's Trump Card.

Is President Trump God's Trump Card?

So many people trusted, per emails received: *It is President Trump ... please put a photo on the book cover of President Trump with people praying with and for President Trump.*

President Trump is a key part of God's Trump Card! He is absolutely revealing what must be addressed and what must be done for us to re-capture and re-secure our nation as a blessed nation, returning to our ONE NATION UNDER GOD!

He is not alone within the structure of God's Trump Card.

President Trump clearly walks in faith and he is committed to revealing the truth and righting the wrongs which devastated our nation for many years, for decades, for the past two centuries!

In the midst of completing the research on the key symbols we need to be aware of, our Father 'interrupted' my time of typing. When he does this, I have learned it is best for me to become immediately obedient.

For many reasons I trust Yahweh when He does this!

This time, however, it was very different.

In fact, it was very odd!

Why? Father prompted me to turn on the TV and view the exact moment of a Hallmark film.

At first, I was saying, *Really?* When he actually prompted me to be silent and I heard a line in the film: ***The ancient meaning of Trust is alliance.***

As soon as I heard this statement, our Father immediately informed me that my break time is over! *Really?*

This is all our Father wanted to reveal to me so I would research the word trust. I thought it was merely because I do declare, often, exactly what and whom I trust.

Another lesson learned: TRUST. When trust is granted it means we are expressing confidence in the honesty or integrity of a person or a thing and in ancient times it meant we formed an alliance or a pact by trusting!

Tears when I realized our Father was prompting me to remember the exact moments when He asked me a very simple question, *Do you trust me?*

Without hesitation or taking a breath I said, *Yes, but, I do not think I am qualified ...*

At that time, I did not realize what I just learned. In the moment, I was forming an alliance by saying *Yes* to the question of trust but, it was tearful to realize I broke the alliance, the pact, in the exact same moment by questioning my qualifications because HE calls and qualifies those HE calls.

It is clearly evident our Father has called our President Trump!

When our President first declared FAKE NEWS, even though I had lived through years of false ID reports and false stories made up by people who say different information 'on paper' and they did not know who I really was 'in person', even I questioned this status.

Even I wondered what would happen based upon that term being shared, in large part because I knew a lot of the reasons why the term was actually the truth before it was accepted by the public and yet, the public believed the lies within the FAKE NEWS.

However, the shock of the term being stated repeatedly is exactly what began the process of waking up millions of people, in America and globally, to the fact the news is being presented to keep us encased in a web of deceit. In a term our Father would use, we were being enslaved by many who operate in evil, without our

179

knowledge or our consent. <u>We were in bondage without realizing the deceit.</u>

Father forgive us!

We have lived with the full knowledge of the power and authority granted to us while we are truly joint-heirs with Christ and yet, we have sometimes aligned with idols and we have allowed generations to make idols of people, entertainer, athletes, things of the world declared to have great value, and events, and we did not know their plan or intent until the evil acts were made known to us in current days. Reveal unto us this day any thing the enemy is using against us and any way we have aligned with the evil doers in this world.

Praising You, Father, for never leaving or forsaking us while we walk forward in faith and depart from the plan in the world which You confirmed will come to naught!

Thank you, Father for re-aligning us with Your plan, Your will so Your will and plan will be done as You have ordained.

Thank You, Father, for providing a man of God to stand firm against the depth of evil which has overtaken the leadership in the government of our nation. Many within the government have aligned with the deceiver so we thank You for opening the eyes and ears of all in government, local, regional, state and federal, of all who will hear Your voice in these days! We stand together as Your TRUMP CARD in this generation and proclaim aligned with President Trump that the evil shall end now & never be allowed to control & manipulate the people, especially those in all levels of leadership within the government, in business, in the many facets of our economy, our trade, tariffs and commerce, our travel, our sports, our laws or banking system, ever again!

GOD's Trump Card

Now, you are realizing the Trump Card God has sent to earth is <u>US</u>! Powerful because HE sent us, because HE loves the people 'in the world' so much, he knew if it was going to become on earth as it is in heaven, HE had to send <u>us</u> to proceed upon our assignments in these days *For The Sake Of America* and for all believers globally!

We are becoming witnesses to the return of the believers to their first love, to the ONLY LIVING LORD, to the Divine Law as granted to us in the WORD!

Our Father knew exactly when it was the time *FOR THE SAKE OF AMERICA* to send you to earth with your assignment, for you to be able to fulfill upon your purpose and plan in these days so evil would be revealed & rooted OUT of our nation, of our Constitution, a document which was established per the Divine Law of the Bible. Father knew we would stand firm until it is restored with the commitment of the people to NOT LET EVIL OVERTAKE OUR LIFE, OUR FAMILY OR OUR NATION!

HE knew we would not stop until the evil was dealt with!

Our Father began this promise when He sent His Son!

He loved us so much He sent His Son to re-encourage the tribes of Israel and to usher in the Holy Spirit until HE returns!

He loved us so much He sent Donald J Trump to earth at the exact time to become our President, a President who will not be compromised and he is not able to be blackmailed.

Our Father sent him to earth at the exact right time!

The wisdom our Father has granted to our President is evident. The ability to remain energized with only four hours of sleep each night while keeping up the amazing schedule is another sign of 'walking in faith with our Father'!

Often, I have reminded myself 'out loud' with our Father when I realize the prayers have gone on through the midnight hour wherever HE has placed my feet on the soil of the world ... *if I can have more than 3.5 hours of sleep, I will rest. If not, I will remain 'in rest with You', in Your word and prayer.*

Both options restore & refresh for what our Father is laying out before me or before us! His plans are mighty and HE already knows we are qualified!

My nightly prayer confirms this fact: *Thank You for putting me into deep rest in Your presence this night and waking me when You need me.*

It's a human thing but, if I have a critical flight time or meeting time the next morning, I will automatically set an alarm. It's a habit!

Trusting, again, I operate in a way which makes our Father laugh because he always wakes me, typically seven minutes before the alarm time I set, with HIS full knowledge! I may not smile the moment my eyes open and I realize what HE has done for me but, I know that I know He loves me this much and HE has proven to me again and again that HE has a tremendous, timely and accurate sense of humor!

Critical for us to accept, there is a 'Master Plan' for each of us and we are here to live it out while 'on earth'. IF we ignore or proceed in disobedience (or procrastination, both of which are sins!), we may miss out on the opportunity of a lifetime!

Exactly as our Father had a plan for us, sent us to earth at the exact, right time, our Father sent President Donald J Trump to earth with the plan which is unfolding now laid out before him, a plan unfolding with amazing accuracy from the exact moment he arrived.

President Trump was born exactly **700 days** before Israel was re-formed as a nation. Therefore, when Israel was **77 days old**, President Trump was exactly **777** days old.

On election day in America, 2016, Israel's Prime Minister Benjamin Netanyahu was exactly **seventy (70) years, seven (7) months and seven (7) days old.**

183

On inauguration day in America, on January 20, 2017, President Trump was sworn in when he was exactly (**70**) **years, seven (7) months and seven (7) days old.**

Vice President Pence was **57 years old.**

Israel was **70 years old.**

All of this happened in the Hebrew calendar year: **5777.**

Our Father loved His people so much He sent you!

Breathe!

Take in another, deep breath of life from our Father!

Let all of the 'stuff' go as you exhale.

Then, take in another deep breath of life!

Our Father is as close as the next breath He gives us!

Our Father operates in 'exact plans and dates'.

Everything about you was known before you arrived.

Yes. You have free will. You can do whatever you want while you are 'on earth'. You can operate with the world, align with the enemy. The choice is yours. Our Father will NOT control you while His desire is that you will NOT depart from him!

His love is unconditional.

He understands human nature.

He knows we may feel like turning and running away.

However, He is our rear guard and HE wants us to go forward!

He gives us second chances!

He gave a second chance to Adam: **Genesis 3:22.** Then the **Lord** God said, *"Behold, the man has become like one of Us, to know good and evil. And now, <u>lest he put out his hand and take also of the tree of life, and eat, and live forever"</u>* —

PAUSE … the pause did not change the status because Adam did not repent, did not seek counsel … Adam departed.

Tesla. Now you are ready to hear the great details!

Do you know the middle name of our President Donald J Trump? The J stands for John.

Dr. John G Trump was the brother of Fred Trump, the uncle of our President Donald J Trump. When you have a few moments, you will enjoy viewing the biography information about the MIT research engineer, Dr. John G Trump.

<u>Providing a little clue</u>: The US government invited Dr. Trump to review the papers remaining after the death of Tesla. Trusting you can realize why I asked you to review the 52 pages of the April 2007 Idaho Observer article by reporter Don Nicoloff.

What the world did with malice of forethought.

Wow, Father just downloaded that phrase and then prompted me to look up the definition: **malice** aforethought. n. 1) the conscious intent to cause death or great bodily harm to another person before a person commits the crime. Such **malice** is a required element to prove first degree murder. 2) a general evil and depraved state of mind in which the person is unconcerned for the lives of others.

Our Father has a counter plan!

Sat with this statement for a while as I have never used the term and I did not know why our Father wanted me to insert it!

Does it fit? What happened to Tesla and how our LORD is turning it all around? YES!

But, what is the scriptural reference? I am always asked for the scriptural reference so I went right back to our Father!

Promise not to laugh?

Malice of forethought is in scripture!

GOD's humor has such depth!

His training, through His messages to me, is a precious process of turning me into a bible quoting believer (not a scholar)!

Numbers 35:16-21. *'But if he strikes him with an iron implement, so that he dies, he is a murderer; the murderer shall surely be put to death. 17 And if he strikes him with a stone in the hand, by which one could die, and he does die, he is a*

186

murderer; the murderer shall surely be put to death. **18** *Or if he strikes him with a wooden hand weapon, by which one could die, and he does die, he is a murderer; the murderer shall surely be put to death.* **19** *The avenger of blood himself shall put the murderer to death; when he meets him, he shall put him to death.* **20** *If he pushes him out of hatred or, while lying in wait, hurls something at him so that he dies,* **21** *or in enmity he strikes him with his hand so that he dies, the one who struck him shall surely be put to death. He is a murderer. The avenger of blood shall put the murderer to death when he meets him.*

The WORD often refers to the term!

Within scripture, the term also has another link to our laws, divine and American, due to realizing premeditated murder is the EXACT SAME THING!

Premeditated murder is what happened to Tesla!

Wow, GOD!

It all lines up with the Tesla portion of the article by the investigative reporter, Don Nicoloff!

Counterfeit plan of the enemy uses 'defeat' as a judgment upon us, as though the enemy can give us a 'life sentence'!

LIAR! LIAR! LIAR!

WE ARE NOT TO ALIGN WITH THE ENEMY!

The song by Danny Gokey is repeatedly going through my mind: RISE!

No matter what LIE the LIAR is whispering or screaming in your ear, listen to your CREATOR, He wants to restore your glory so RISE!

You were made to RISE!

LIES in using scripture as a reason for EVIL to unfold:

Skull and Crossbones use 3:22 as their symbol.

The evil structure supports the fact the enemy wants us to think we were defeated in the garden and the enemy won!

LIAR!

The Georgia Guidestones were erected on 3/22 on purpose!

They are 19 feet tall.

The Georgia Guidestones are promoted as the tallest granite monument.

The Faith Monument is 81 feet tall.

LIES!

They are counterfeit stones!

Their evil statements are LIES, only some words of the LIAR!

We are witnessing # 7 of the 10 Georgia Guidestones:

Avoid Petty Laws and Useless Officials.

IT IS TIME FOR US, We The People, TO RISE!

SEEK TRUTH

Humble Ourselves

Operate as Christ directed:

Only what we Hear our Father Say, Do what He Does!

STOP LIVING THE LIES OF 4th & 5th CENTURIES:

Paganism was merged with Christian truth in 312-325 AD which would be the Fourth Century.

Pythian belief structure, prevalent since the Fifth Century!

New meaning to an old term: *Nothing new under the sun.*

Do you suppose it was ALL done to focus ALL who knew the truth to ONLY proceed with the WRONG facts which results in sun god worship?

It is what was done FOR CENTURIES to 'control the people'.

In the midst of the deep, deep web of deceit research our Father wanted me to click on a YouTube video to the right of the one He told me to view.

There was a little bit of resistance because He directed me to the video I was still watching.

However, I complied and I was shocked!

It is the biography about King Louis the XIV.

Why did GOD want me to view the video?

King Louis XIV was also known as 'The Sun King'!

WHAT?

1700 years of 'mixed up information'.

Paganism = sun god worship and it 'is the structure' of life.

NOT understanding or honoring the truth regarding our history, our heritage, our blessed position as a joint heir for the past 1700 years!

The HEBREW calendar, the feasts and festivals were not the basis of the calendar. In fact, they were NOT inserted so we have not followed our language or our culture, the truth confirmed by Christ when HE walked on the earth and DEMONSTRATED truth.

Christ did not compromise.

Christ turned over the tables.

Christ spoke truth to the Pharisees and the Sadducees.

A dear sister in Christ, Rebecca King, shared a great status of where we are today and it also confirms EXACTLY what Christ experienced: *They are not FAIR YOU SEE and that is so SAD YOU SEE.*

That phrase said it all to me!

TRUTH: Christ did not align with the words of the enemy (including the Pharisees and the Sadducees).

Christ did not hesitate, HE took the keys from the enemy.

Christ demonstrated LIFE to us and sacrificed ALL for us to have life and be able to live 'free on the land'!

Christ confirmed the Holy Spirit would come and we would always be able to communicate direct.

Peter confirmed the promise: **Acts 2:38-39.** Then Peter said unto them, ***Repent, and be baptized every one of you in the name of Jesus Christ for the remission of sins, and ye shall receive the gift of the Holy Ghost.***

The body of believers have not aligned with the Holy Spirit and united as believers. The only way we will be able to retain Liberty and Freedom is with the counsel of the Father, daily!

When we do not have the words, the Holy Spirit language (speaking in tongues) is the communication which expresses the request from our heart, where Christ resides, direct to our Father.

When Father sent me on a seven day journey *In Search Of Wigglesworth*, he shared a vision at the end of the journey.

Insert from *In Search Of Wigglesworth*

The LORD's Vision About Revival

While I was expressing my upset after realizing the people do not remember all the LORD had done in the region, and in the Hebrides and Azusa Street at the same time, I was immediately surrounded by His glory, standing with Him in a very light and bright place.

Lots of lights were shining bright.

It took a moment to realize I was in a hospital, just inside the Emergency room entrance. This provided a view of all the activity coming in from the world.

When the Emergency room doors opened, ambulances were backed up at the entrance with their back doors wide open.

Each ambulance carried what appeared to be an identical 'little white wood church'. Each church was on a gurney. Doctors were confirming the status: *Dead On Arrival,* since each church had flat lined.

Each one of the emergency staff waited for a different doctor or a team of doctors to show up, to 'revive the church/patient'.

Workers were everywhere, waiting on the expert team, but, before the 'blue cart' team could get to the gurney more and more ambulances were arriving. The ambulances could not even get near the emergency room doors, since additional ambulances were already lined up at the entrance. As each paramedic opened the back doors of the ambulance, it was clear they were delivering another church to be revived.

In that moment (I have no idea how long I observed this status) the LORD confirmed: *"This is the condition of My people, My church. This is why I sent you to search for Wigglesworth. The heart is where Christ resides. The Holy Spirit guides in truth, strengthening where and when the people are weak."*

I was stunned, speechless. Wow.

The visual was effective.

This is the condition of our church, today.

This is how the church appears to God, with the health of the church in jeopardy.

Then, I cried out to God: *Lord, what will it take to remind the people about a region known as Sunderland, England, and help them remember how the people were touched while You sent an illiterate man, Wigglesworth, around the world?*

God revealed the sad status of the body of Christ.

It hit my heart like a ton of bricks!

God's confirmations were tearful as I was hearing the truth from the people which matched the words upon God's heart: *"The people do not remember."*

At the time of the vision, I had no idea God was actually tapping me on the shoulder to share the truth about *Restoration vs. Revival* with the body of Christ.

Bottom line: *God's plan does not to require reviving our 'flat lined' heart! We have life in Christ and He resides in our heart!*

If you have not read *It's A Faith Walk!* you are not aware of the levels of resistance God has dealt with since it's not always been easy for God to deal with me. I have often reminded God that I'm merely a farmer's daughter from Nebraska, as if God did not know my entire history before he sent me forth!

Trusting in this moment our LORD, our Father, is doing all He can to tap you on the shoulder for God's plans are BIG for each of us. It is typical to resist, to not feel worthy.

The question is: Will you respond? Will your answer be Yes? Will you do whatever it takes to encourage and restore another believer? Will you do all you can to not become discouraged? If so, enjoy this reminder the LORD gave to me:

If it takes 1000 people to touch one person's heart, you may only be number 575 or 999 so you do not see results. Do not become discouraged, the fact is you touched the heart and that is what matters.

If you are not sure you are operating in the full power and authority of the Holy Spirit, yet, this simple prayer will help:

Father I am declaring Christ is my Savior and I am asking in this moment for the Holy Spirit to fully enter into me, so I will be filled now and with full surrender to You I desire to express the evidence of speaking in tongues, so I can communicate with you without trying to express myself by using 'earthly words' for it is my desire to operate in full power and authority in my life from this moment forward!

LIES have to be countered! Holy Spirit takes over when we cry out to the Father, even when we do not have 'earthly words' to do so!

Where we are weak, our Father is strong!

We are never alone.

We will NOT be operating by ourselves again 'in the heat of the battle' <u>unless we chose to proceed and 'do it in our own power'</u>!

We need our Father's help to do it, to gain HIS wisdom, to become as wise as the serpent, to discern truth, to counter the enemy, the counterfeit 'on earth', in the moment, on a daily basis.

Hebrew calendar does not align with the calendar we use. Hebrew feasts and festivals align with our history and culture while they do not align with the pagan dates celebrated as

Christian dates 'on earth', Christmas is NOT a Christian holiday – honors the pagan sun gods (there is a list!), or the pagan child sacrifice day of Ishtar (Easter in English) when their blood is used to dye eggs. All Hallowed Eve is the eve before All Hallowed Day.

The Hebrew calendar does not match the weekly structure or the annual counting of days as the world based calendar.

There is much for us to learn, and then align with going forward. As the children's program answers the question: *Can We Do It?* **YES WE CAN!**

Father forgive us!

We did not plan on aligning with the enemy.

We did not know the truth direct from You and Your word.

We spent time hearing the words of humans and we aligned and trusted without seeking confirmation of the words from You.

Thank You, Father, for keeping Your hand upon us, for not forsaking us, and for giving us second chances!

We desire a second chance for this nation, for the return to a blessed nation as ONE NATION UNDER GOD and we stand firm for the believer's globally to seek Your truth and align with You in these days for we realize You formed us in Your image and You prepared us for the assignment 'on earth' before the foundation of the earth. We promise to no longer consider the plan to be bigger than we can comprehend or take on and accomplish as Your Ambassadors while we are 'on earth'. Our desire is to proceed upon the purpose and plan You have laid out before us, uniting together in Your truth while accomplishing the assignment we were given for these exact days, trusting You and the plan!

Uniting together in truth and sharing the truth generation to generation is the only way the reforming of our nation and the body of believers to the true plan in these days will be retained and sustained, and passed on to the third and fourth generations by each generation.

In the depth of the debacle I experienced with the top government agents, a depth of deception beyond the debacle I experienced in the judicial system and brought to the attention of the agents' I learned the value of the deep, daily desire to repent and hear the truth direct from our Father through the Holy Spirit.

Perfection is not achieved, yet. However, my moments of questioning are shorter and shorter with each message and vision received from our Father. Praying I will always remain surrendered to HIS plan, HIS will and HIS assignment for me 'while on earth' so I will hear HIM say, *Well done, good and faithful servant!*

The experiences taught me the deep love of our Father, a love which does pass ALL UNDERSTANDING.

Our Father's love does not change based upon what we are experiencing 'in the moment'.

Whatever the situation is, we only need to call upon HIM and invite HIM into our situation for we are HIS! And, HE knows what we do NOT know, because HE knows the end from the beginning!!!

Jeremiah 29:11. *For I know the plans I have for you,"* declares the **LORD**, *"plans to prosper you and not to harm you, plans to give you hope and a future.*

In the depth of despair, I learned again and again, and again, the promises of our Father remain: *We are more than conquerors! We are the head and NOT the tail!* I heard this so often from prayer partners while my situation did NOT change, I actually found myself mocking the words as though they could not be true because I could not see the change, yet!

It took me a while to realize the truth, the change needed to happen IN ME!

Wow! It was a process of expanding my faith, declaring the promises of God from scripture!

John 14:18. *I will not leave you comfortless: I will come to you.*

He will come!

Will we go to Him?

Will we align with Him?

Will we honor Him for who He is, and what He has done and who He has become for us?

1. **Reverential fear! Before Christ, believers desired to live in reverential fear of the only true GOD. Divine Protection was granted to warriors, leaders, kings who sought the Father and held themselves in true commitment to the Father. Divine Protection was granted!**

2. **Salvation through Christ! Living by the grace of our Father as a joint-heir with Christ! Divine Protection is granted!**

A few examples of divine protection in my life are included within the books, especially in *It's A Faith Walk!*

Divine Protection of leaders in our nation include a significant example confirmed by the testimony of a warrior, a chief who commanded his warriors to focus upon killing the early American military leaders since it would cause the troops to scatter.

President Washington was an Officer and later, a General. During the battle, he was an officer, a leader of a troop.

The focus of the plan to kill the leaders did not produce the result! After being shot multiple times by multiple warriors, including the chief, the chief halted the effort.

The chief recognized the status because he knew the meaning of Divine Protection granted due to holding reverential fear himself, he knew the value of life by honoring our Father.

Divine Protection of our Father upon the life of the military officer, Washington, resulted in the chief choosing to end the battle that day.

Divine Protection caused the chief to make the long journey to meet the mighty warrior of GOD, Washington, in person 15 years later when he declared the journey was tough for such an old man.

The testimony is covered in great detail within *For The Sake Of America II.*

Now that we recognize the truth, I pray we will choose to operate in the truth, for the truth reveals the enemy plans are not able to defeat us. Battle is over before we think it begins!

Christ took the keys from the enemy and released the believers before ascending to heaven.

Christ shed His blood for our protection and our eternal salvation.

The question is personal, do we believe, do we actually trust?

When we form the alliance, the pact in trusting our Father, it protects us while the plan of the enemy remains the same.

The enemy does not have a new game plan!

The enemy will keep using the exact same tactics, day after day: **Fear, Doubt & Unbelief** in his attempt to **Steal, Kill and Destroy.** As our Father confirmed to me, *If you choose to 'dance with the devil' it will continues until he tires you and you stop ...*

WE ARE HERE TO WALK FORWARD IN FAITH ...
Therefore, the choice to trust our Father and remain in truth as HIS Trump Card is a daily decision to *Always Speak Life.*

You are a warrior, and our Father knows you will do well!

Proverbs 22:6.
Train up a child in the way he should go,
And when he is old he will not depart from it.
You are in great company!

Believers globally are waking up, standing firm and getting into position to fulfill upon the purpose and plan in these days *FOR THE SAKE OF AMERICA.* The body of believers globally are praising and singing and letting the world know they are warriors of the ONLY LIVING LORD and VICTORY is ours!

II Chronicles 7:14. *if My people who are called by My name will humble themselves, and pray and seek My face, and turn from their wicked ways (REPENT), then I will hear from heaven, and will forgive their sin and heal their land (RESTORE).*

In Hong Kong, the protesters are singing praise worship songs. Student protesters were singing: *Sing Hallelujah to the LORD* Wow!

A clear difference from the student protests at universities across America from citizens who have the rights and freedoms Hong Kong students are losing due to Britain turning control on Hong Kong back to China. Their rights and freedoms were to be protected but, that is not what they are experiencing.

What are they doing to re-gain their rights and freedoms, to turn their situation around? They are inviting the LORD into their situation, remaining united as believers who gained religious freedom, while praying and praising the LORD for they KNOW one thing to be TRUE, the LORD will not leave them or forsake them.

In America, people who think they are required to protest in America do not realize the truth. They are not seeking wisdom. They are following along, whether naive or innocent to an evil plan. They are aligning with organizations established with evil intent and proceeding upon an evil plan.

Praying when the layers of evil hidden from many due to being encased within the web of deceit filled with significant plans to steal, kill and destroy from legal citizens, believers, for so many decades, the American people will wake up and unite together.

There is only one truth.

Much of what we have heard from the *Mockingbird Media* was only shared to keep us from knowing the truth.

Father forgive us!

Praying we will seek the truth direct from our Father for HE is our protector, HE is our rear guard, HE has plans laid our before each of us to live an abundant life and prosper.

Food for thought: On the 29th of October, 2019, it will be the 90th Anniversary of the Stock Market Crash.

The crash was planned by those who were already operating within their plan for the centralized bank to control America. The 'banking crisis' handled by J P Morgan 'without oversight' in 1907 already resulted in banks being declared insolvent ONLY by the decision of J P Morgan.

At the time, the decision was already made to proceed with a candidate for President they knew they could control at the conclusion of the second term of President Theodore Roosevelt. Roosevelt was a big problem for the 'elite' because he declared and decreed the Republic would be honored and the government and the people operate together in unity.

What does 90 mean in Hebrew:

The hand of GOD's discipline

90   Saints Sifted

10 X 9 Testimony X Judgment

IF this book is released on Yom Kippur, as the prior books in the series, on October 9, the crash anniversary is 20 days later, October 29.

What does 20 mean in Hebrew: REDEMPTION

Praying We The People will accept being God's Trump Card, gather together NOW as a body of believers with full faith and pray specifically for GOD's divine protection for us, for our families, for America, for our President and for ALL in leadership who are operating in truth! May all be revealed to us about those who are NOT operating in truth so we will continue to pray without ceasing until ALL who are given the leadership opportunity will seek truth and serve the people in truth!

AMEN ... OUR GOD IS A FAITHFUL KING!

Acts 5:38. And now I say to you, keep away from these men and let them alone; for if this plan or this work is of men, it will come to nothing 39 but if it is of God, you cannot overthrow it – lest you even be found to fight against God.

500 year plan.

The Pilgrims established a 500 year plan.

IF the plan began upon arrival in 1620, the plan would proceed with all 'living free, in peace on the land' until 2120.

They followed God's plan to live in liberty and freedom for 500 years. We did not remain aligned with the plan for 200 years!

America is not 'in trouble' due to a couple of political decisions such as the previous administration or the removal of prayer from public schools. We allowed change. We aligned with other choices!

The Tribes of Israel, the sons of Jacob / Israel, had a choice to make, to either remain enslaved in Assyria or proceed to the uninhabited land GOD provided.

They followed the plan of our Father, the Creator.

They walked for 18 months, guided by our Father.

The tribes remained 'in peace', governed by Divine Law, living on the land of abundance GOD provided from about 500 (or 600) BC until the 1800's! They arrived and were living on the land 2000 years before it became America, a time period within the stone age.

What did they etch on the stone?

The Ten Commandments & Praise be to Yah!

Ark of the Covenant carried into Battle!

The Seven Feasts & Festivals Honored!

This is why our history is recorded by them in ancient Paleo Hebrew upon stone, exactly as we found with the Ten Commandments and a 10th century BC artifact preserved and donated to the Cherokee Museum in Cherokee, North Carolina.

These artifacts confirm the Hebrew language was preserved from the ancient Paleo Hebrew whether they were brought to America by the 'Lost Tribes of Israel' or they were prepared by them once they arrived.

500-600 BC to 1800 AD.

Peace was retained in a land not called America until 1492.

From the Stone Age to Modern History (started in 1453), peace was preserved on the land named America by Columbus in 1492.

What was happening globally?

1455 Pope confirmed reading first printed bible; small part of the current bible as the New Testament was not added until 1500's.

1492 Columbus arrived with the exiled Jews who escaped from Spain. Jews had experienced severe persecution from Spain before they journeyed to the new land. Dark Ages / Middle Ages, a time period which began in the fifth century AD with the collapse of the Roman Empire and continued until 1453, transitioned to the current time period referred to as Modern History.

1517 Martin Luther posted the 95 theses; bible still in German. Martin Luther posted the theses based upon his anger with Pope Leo X's new round of 'indulgences' (good works or payments to cancel out sins; described by Luther as corrupting people's faith) to help build St. Peter's Basilica.

Luther hoped the points would lead to an open discussion. Copies spread throughout the region within two weeks, throughout Europe within two months. Results: Luther was excommunicated from the Catholic Church.

1535 William Tyndale translated the bible direct from Hebrew and Greek texts. Published copies were smuggled into England by merchants. **(DVD: *God's Outlaw,* Tyndale's life story)**

Pilgrims / Puritans taught their children the Lord's Prayer and scriptures in English.

1536 King Henry VIII was counseled that the people would become independent of the monarchy if the bible became available in English. People were imprisoned and burned at the stake for possessing a bible or speaking scriptures in English, including the martyrs involved with Tyndale and then, Tyndale in 1536.

King Henry VIII approved a bible for distribution within three years of executing Tyndale, in 1539.

1539 bible version includes most of the Tyndale bible translation while all credit was given to Myles Coverdale.

1611 King James bible was distributed. This version included the Apocrypha; remained until 1835 when it was removed by the British & Foreign Bible Society. The society was formed in 1804.

207

Coincidence?

Life changed for the 'Lost Tribes of Israel', the Native American Indians in 1804, also. Treaty signings were frequent with the transfer of significant parcels of land to the 'new government'. The Native Americans knew no deeds were to be in 'human names' because all of the land belongs to our Father.

Native Indian Removal Act in 1830; forced to leave their homes and land (1831-1850) even though the Cherokee won their case in the Supreme Court.

Shortly after the Native American Indians were removed from their homes and their land through the Indian Removal Act in 1830, two years after gold was discovered in Georgia, 1828, the British and Foreign Bible Society removed the Apocrypha in 1835!

Coincidence?

People in England were still being imprisoned and burned at the stake for studying the English bible, meeting in groups separate from the Church of England. Residents were still being forced to attend the Church of England.

People were not allowed to miss services of the Church of England (formerly the Catholic Church until King Henry required changes to marry and divorce to marry who he wanted to marry).

In fact, when Puritans (purely follow the bible 'as is') were found in homes or public locations sharing the bible and meeting to fellowship, they were arrested and imprisoned. This status continued even after Pilgrims/Puritans left England the first time. They were imprisoned before their second departure.

1604 Pilgrims began their plan to depart from England. The journey is traced within a DVD by Kirk Cameron, *Monumental.*

1620 Pilgrims arrive at Plymouth Rock.

Pilgrims made a choice to sacrifice everything, including their assets, their friends, family and even their life, with nearly half of the Pilgrims dying during the first winter before they joined the inhabitants on the new land known as America.

Pilgrims lived 'in peace' with the Native Indians and the Jews from Spain. How? They were able to 'live in peace', aligned together in the 'same truth' with the 500 year plan established to live in and retain liberty and freedom for the current & future generations.

They remained in peace with the Indians and Jews 'on the land' and operated in truth, sharing from the LORD's abundance of provision. Native Indians shared everything with the Jews when they arrived from Spain in 1492, and again when the Pilgrims arrived in 1620 AD.

Native Indians retained peace together through the arrival of Europeans in greater and greater numbers in the 1700's, after living free on the land for about 2300 years. They knew and lived according to GOD's Divine Law. They knew GOD's provision would be 'more than enough' during the establishment of the Colonies until 1732 when Georgia was structured as the last colony in 1732.

Native Indians lived in peace and shared the abundance from the land for more than 2000 years before the Jews arrived and for more than 100 years before the Pilgrims arrived because they knew their Creator and the Great Spirit. <u>They passed on the truth about GOD's provision and how the people 'in the bible' lived without having a 'printed bible' to refer to</u>! Wow! 2300 years of retaining peace and sharing truth changed within less 100 years! In fact, in less than 60 years.

By 1830, an American law was passed, a Native Indian Removal Act. The very people who inhabited the land for 2300 years were removed in less than 100 years from the Colonies being fully established with their help.

Within 50 years after they participated in the battles to help America become an independent nation, they were ordered to leave their homes and land. What a bizarre "Jubilee" (50 year increment) for them!

Pattern of 'what happened' to America after Native Indians were living in truth and peace on the land for more than 2000 years is briefly summarized as follows:

100 Years
1500-1600

1492 – 1604 / 1620

Jews from Spain arrived. They escaped persecution, loss of homes and assets, imprisonment and death. Pilgrims joined with the next generations, continuing GOD's plan, living in truth and peace, retaining freedom and liberty, after they were persecuted, parents put to death or imprisoned.

100 Years
1600-1700

1620 – 1732 (Georgia became a Colony)

Colonies are formed along the East Coast of America.

Founding documents for the Colonies and America were structured with the Native Indians and Pilgrims based upon Divine Law.

Pilgrims, Jews from Spain and Native Indians lived in peace.

100 Years
1700-1800

1732 (Georgia became a Colony) - 1830

The Native Indians, Jews & Pilgrims were united in their faith. They established the exact process we were to continue to follow to remain in liberty and freedom as defined within the 500 year plan to keep America united in Faith, living in Liberty and Freedom as structured within the Faith Monument pillars, exactly as the Native Indians preserved it for nearly 2200-2300 years before Europeans arrived in great numbers and changed some founding documents established for America.

The plan is clearly stated on the four pillars of the Faith Monument which was built and paid for by our Congress, dedicated in 1889, more than 100 years after we became an independent nation in 1776.

1828 Gold was discovered in Georgia and the Native Indians were forced out of their homes and off of their land due to a new law: **Native Indian Removal Act** which passed by one vote.

1830 Native Indians were 'forced out' of their homes and from their land and legally forced to proceed upon the Trail of Tears.

The tears were for those who committed the crimes and atrocities, those who remained on the land GOD gave to the Native Indians.

Tears shed for the enmity Native Indians knew the 'new residents' created, trusting the 'new residents' knew not what they were 'putting into motion' between them as the new 'residents upon the land' and the Father, the Creator.

100 Years
1776-1889

1776 / 1781-3 – 1889

We focus upon July 4, 1776 as our date of becoming independent from Britain. However, GOD kept drawing my attention to 1781. Research for this date was fascinating!

1781 There was a war I was not aware of: ***Southern War Phase of the Revolutionary War.*** This war is considered to be the second half of the Revolutionary War.

The War involved Virginia, North and South Carolina, Georgia, East and West Florida. while the Revolutionary War continued as a War in the South, with the American War of Independence until September 3, 1783.

Bibles paid for by individual members of Congress, signers of the Independence with more than 50% obtaining seminary degrees.

1861 – 1865 Civil War; War Between The States.

The South KNEW the direction of the nation was already headed in the wrong direction.

The plans against the nation, the Native Americans, confirmed the plans for this blessed nation were being changed by the 'new people' entering the nation.

1889 Faith Monument dedication in 1889.

100 Years
1800-1900

1804 – 1907 / 1910 / 1913

1804 Treaties for peace were arranged with the Native Indians for large parcels of land across America to operate 'in peace' while the land was taken over by new residents upon the land.

1907 President Theodore Roosevelt was 'on a hunt' while a banking crisis was declared and J P Morgan selected which banks survived the crisis; President Roosevelt retained American Government as our Republic.

1910 Federal Reserve was established, structured as an entity.

1913 President Woodrow Wilson inaugurated. Within days: Constitutional Amendments 16 & 17 approved.

16   Enacted Federal Reserve and the IRS.

IRS established to collect taxes; 1st time, a Fed tax.

17   Senators changed to popular vote status.

No longer 'selected' by representatives.

No longer able to be removed for not representing the people and replaced with those who will.

Counters our ability to remove those who do not represent us (Senators are to represent the interests of their State) and replace them with those who will represent us (from our Representatives).

Senators are to represent state interests but, they changed to represent global interests. They have also become people who are not landowners, etc., as required within the constitution so they have a 'stake' they are interested in protecting as a landowner and business owner. Political interests replaced interests of the State they represent. Within weeks and months:

Removed Ambassador to Mexico.

Re-negotiated Treaty with Mexico.

Changed American structure from Republic to Democracy.

Proceeded with an extensive 'Progressive Agenda'.

Established League of Nations; United Nations.

Involved with (credited for) Treaty of Versailles.

President Wilson given Nobel Peace Prize for the Treaty.

Leaders in the world were removed; WWI & WWII.

Actions and lies drew Americans into WWI & WWII.

(Leaders have been removed in many nations, since WWII)

100 Years
1830-1930

1830 – 1930

1830 American Government removed Native Indians from their homes and land.

Feds forced 17,000 from homes, marched to Oklahoma!

Gold had been discovered in Georgia in 1828, resulting in a Democrat-controlled Congress rushing through the Indian Removal Act, which passed by a single vote in 1830. It was signed by Democrat President Andrew Jackson and carried out by Democrat President Martin Van Buren.

Over 12,000 Cherokees signed a petition in protest of the Indian Removal Act. Condemning the Federal Government's mandate were members of the National Republican Party and the Whig Party, including: Rep. Abraham Lincoln, Senator Henry Clay, Senator Daniel Webster and Congressmen Davy Crockett.

The Cherokee were largely Christian and even had their own language and alphabet, created in 1821 by Cherokee silversmith Sequoyah.

Christian missionaries led resistance to the Federal Government's removal of the Indians, with many missionaries being arrested by the State of Georgia and sentenced to years of hard labor. Some were arrested for their opposition to Indian removal and their case went to the U.S. Supreme Court.

Chief Justice John Marshall ruled in favor of the Cherokee in Worcester v. Georgia (1832), writing that *the Cherokee*

Nation was a "distinct community" with self-government "in which the laws of Georgia can have no force. "

He (also) said, *"Thanks be to GOD, the Court can wash their hands clean of the iniquity of oppressing the Indians and disregarding their rights. "*

Noting that the Supreme Court had no power to enforce its edicts, but had to rely on the President to actually implement them, Democrat President Jackson was attributed with saying: *"John Marshall has made his decision; now let him enforce it! "*

James Murray shared this summary and he credits this research to an organization established by Bill Federer, facts which are chronicled through a web site: American minute.

The Native American Indians knew the truth and 'lived in truth and peace' from about 500 BC to 1500 AD after Jews arrived from Spain and peace continued another 200 years, with the Pilgrims 100 years after 1620 and settlers arriving in the early 1700's.

Indians knew about the land, the language, the seven feasts, ten commandments, the truth about Noah/Nuah, Tower of Babel, etc.

They knew the truth about the law and GOD's plan.

1930 American Government proceeded with policies and laws resulting in:

1. Bank closures,

2. 1929 Stock Market crash,

3. Home and land foreclosures, forcing families out of their homes and off their land; Dust Bowl followed from 1930-1936.

100 Years: 1889 - 1980

1889 Faith Monument dedicated, above Plymouth Rock.

500 year plan 'carved in stone' to help until 2120.

However, Native Indians already removed 1830-1850.

1980 Georgia Guidestones, dedicated.

Coincidence?

New **BRICS** financial structure 2010 matches languages.

Global and ancient languages.

Eugenics and culling planned against the people.

President Roosevelt repeatedly reminded Americans:

The first requisite of a good citizen in this Republic of ours is that he shall be able and willing to pull his own weight.
New York, Chamber of Commerce, **1902**

The government is us; we are the government, you and I.
Asheville, North Carolina, **1902**

100 Years: 1907-13 – 2007-8 / 2013

1907 - 1913 – 2007-8 / 2013

1907 America was still a Republic.

1907 While President Theodore Roosevelt was on a hunting trip, J P Morgan Chase worked 'solo' to handle a banking crisis; arranged a program identifying which banks were solvent and which banks were not.

Quote by President Theodore Roosevelt, 1910

Our country, this great republic, means nothing unless it means the triumph of a real democracy, the triumph of popular government, and, in the long run, of an economic system under which each man shall be guaranteed the opportunity to show the best that there is in him. Osawatomie, Kansas, 1910

1910 Federal Reserve established.

1913 President Woodrow Wilson inaugurated; everything in America changed in days, weeks and months. New constitutional amendments passed by Congress within days. Federal Reserve (centralized bank), IRS. Changes nationally and globally within weeks and months.

Warning by President Thomas Jefferson:

If the American people ever allow private banks to control the issue of their currency, first by inflation, then by deflation, the banks and corporations that will grow up around the banks will deprive the people of all property – until their children wake-up homeless on the continent their fathers conquered.

218

WAR, LOSS OF INDUSTRY, ECONOMIC COLLAPSE

2003-2013 Economic collapse 'layers' begin to unfold across America; mortgage industry, businesses and development industry not backed by funding in America. Business and industry closures, home owners, business owners, development industry lose homes, businesses and industries. Overnight, credit lines which were keeping businesses 'in the black' and functioning were pulled which placed the owners even further 'in debt'. Farm families of many generations are forced out of their homes and off their land due to economic collapse; only banks are bailed out, not citizens.

100 Years after President Wilson and Beyond

2013-2019. Truth is being revealed; evil plans uncovered.

The momentum of truth being revealed aligns with the widespread plan for ALL believers to pray for ALL to be revealed.

The evil plans of the enemy are finally being uncovered.

Evil 'of the other kingdom' is being revealed.

Not sure believers are ready, yet, to realize the depth of evil.

Satanic rituals have been performed in the highest levels of leadership and the videos may be revealed to the public, soon very soon. Are we ready?

Dark to Light is unfolding, daily

Will we stand firm for the truth?

We wanted ALL to be revealed.

Will we take action steps so the future will NOT repeat past?

LORD forgive us!

LORD reveal to us everything which requires repentance so we can and our nation can restore!

LORD we will serve you in these days and stand firm in the truth and proclaim Your truth to all who have ears to hear!

LORD open the eyes of our heart, help us to see what is happening and what you are asking us to do to retain liberty and freedom, for we have believed and repeated lies, we have been proceeding as though all is well because 'me and mine are fine'.

LORD help us to see what we have not seen, so we will become people who are called by Your name and proceed by Your voice; help us stop operating as the residents of Sodom and Gomorrah who became 'comfortable' in the world and did not stand firm in truth, live by faith and believe You are the only living LORD!

Thank you LORD for speaking to us in our waking and resting hours so we can hear You even when You whisper.

Thank you LORD for bringing each truth to us to repent for in these days for these are amazing days to serve You!

Thank you LORD for keeping Your hand upon us!

Research

Paul Harvey: If I Were The Devil, 1965

https://www.youtube.com/watch?v=AKk_5XH1AEM

Idaho Observer, April 2007, Operation Paperclip

Otto Skorzeny confessions article by Don Nicoloff

Operation Paperclip book by Annie Jacobsen

YouTube Lecture for book signing

https://www.youtube.com/watch?v=HHs5M3pyd3Q&t=2261s

LIST OF SATANIC HOLIDAYS (SRA)

Calendar provided:
www.angelfire.com/my/sherbear/SRAcalendar.html

TIMELINE Interviews

https://www.youtube.com/watch?v=rnbM0cGUTAU

The Queen's Mother In Law (Royal Family Documentary)

(Mother of Prince Philip, especially at 23 and 29 minutes)

Princess Alice, Queen of Greece until removal during coup,
Born Windsor Castle, the Granddaughter of Queen Victoria

Pythian Society

Knights of Pythia

Biography of Justus Rathbone

Pythian castle tours available in Springfield, Missouri

Oracle of Delphi, Pythia, daughter of Apollo

Apollo, a Greek god, son of Zeus

Diana of Ephesus, Temple of Diana formerly Artemis

Artemis, twin sister of Apollo

Hermes, a Greek god, son of Zeus

Rod of Hermes & Cockatrice

Biography of Albert Pike

Biography of Alice (Evans) Bailey and Foster Bailey

Biography of President Woodrow Wilson

Biography of President Franklin D Roosevelt

Credited President Woodrow Wilson as his mentor

A Personal Note Just Between Us

The journey to this point in time has been a lifetime cycle of experiences which resulted in major 'lessons learned'. Wow. So much of what was personally experienced did not matter until now. Shocking to see the status in 20/20 hindsight, 'in print'.

Can honestly TESTIFY (a great song by Social Club Misfits, featuring Crowder) our Father is 'in the details'!

So many examples while Father is prompting me to insert my testimony about the Kingdom of Tonga. It was my first experience in an independent Kingdom in the world. The King's brother transitioned to heaven while I was on the flight from Sydney, Australia to Fiji to spend the lay-over (the entire night) with the pastor and his family who cried out for someone to stand with him (reason I was in Australia) and then, on to the Kingdom of Tonga.

Significant details, far more than I can insert here, in *It's A Faith Walk.* Therefore, I am going to insert only the testimony about changing a nation for our LORD.

The pastor and prayer team were fasting and praying.

While in Australia, I saw an article by the Minister of Finance, Tasi. The quote stopped me in my tracks: *We Must Change or We Will Die.* As a side-note to the testimony, it is a reminder that we must be careful what we declare: *Life and death is in the power of the tongue.*

The pastor was released from fasting and just walked across the threshold of his home when my host family in Australia called to say I would be on the (once a week) flight to Tonga.

Due to the death of the prince, it was a quiet week, praying here and there with people in the government. My translator, Sela, was precious. Her photo is within the Tonga photos in the acknowledgments section of this book.

When I was down to three days before my departure flight, the weekend, Sela called the pastor and insisted that he call and arrange a meeting with the Minister of Finance because 'what I was sharing with her about our Father' should be shared with him, and if the pastor would not make the call Sela would call the Minister of Finance and arrange an appointment.

If you are wondering why I was in the Kingdom nearly one week without making an appointment. The truth is: No matter what the article stated while I was in Australia, and not matter what the prayer team thought because they were released from fasting and prayer exactly when our Father provided the funds for the flight in a miraculous way, there is nothing for me to say to ANYONE unless our Father arranges the appointment.

Well, within minutes of the call from Sela, the pastor called to say I had an appointment with Tasi, the Minister of Finance, in the morning.

When we arrived, Sela made the introductions for me and for the pastor. Then, the Minister excused her from the meeting.

The Minister was quite tall! He began by motioning for me to be seated across from him and then he put his hands on his hips and sat in a very regal manner. He began sharing his background information. He started with a long list of Universities and and each degree had a different emphasis. Plus, he had extensive bible training! Tears, the Holy Spirit tears which flow over the bottom lid were filling my eyes and preparing to flow down both sides of my face. Trusting it was because I had no idea, yet, what our Father wanted me to say.

Insert # 1 from *It's A Faith Walk!*

Thanking God for taking over when it was time for me to respond. I could only say, *"I've obtained a few degrees, I'm not a bible scholar, but, I trust God has sent me as His servant to serve you ..."* and, when I took a breath I noticed a strange tapping sound.

225

I looked at the pastor; he was in tears. Then, I looked at Minister Tasi and he was in tears. Their tears were falling on their wraps, a wrap which all Tongans wear, and that was making the sound I heard.

Minister Tasi stood up and told me, *"Tomorrow, I will close the offices and our leaders will meet with you. We will fill the room ..."* God took over. It was as though I was swept up in the glory of God in that moment. I was no longer hearing any words or activities of the people around me.

I saw the pastor making schedule arrangements with the staff. I noticed my hand was outstretched and I was shaking hands with the Minister, his staff, and Sela, before departing. I was still not hearing any words from people as I walked to the pastor's car.

The introduction was made by the Holy Spirit. I merely 'showed up'.

This experience was so surreal. To this day, I'm still not able to remember any other details about that meeting. However, God has extended his sense of humor about introductions, because I've been introduced to speak and when a speaker does not appear, I am asked to speak merely because I 'showed up' for the meeting. This has happened on several occasions since my special introduction to Minister Tasi, the Minister of Finance for The Kingdom of Tonga.

Newspaper Headline: Government Office Closed

226

The Honorable Minister of Finance, Tasi, canceled the schedule for the top 30 senior staff of the government the next day. A seminar was provided in the morning and individual coaching for the government leaders was provided in the afternoon, with a specific scripture being shared from the Lord for each man participating. The words were given per the prompting of the Holy Spirit because my bible was already packed in my luggage. God was good to me by giving me the words! It was a full day!

Now, after revealing how the Kingdom gained wisdom on how to change and LIVE, by gaining a VOICE to lead and bless, I am skipping forward to the 'connection' which our Father was orchestrating BEFORE He sent me to the Kingdom of Tonga.

Due to the repeated extensions of seven days, seven times and then seven days in the Kingdom of Tonga, I returned to America thinking I would have a time of 'rest to catch up'. However, that was merely my personal plan. Our Father decided I would be on a flight the next day to London.

Again, our Father arranged for me to be extended seven times for seven days at a time. When I was I Malmo, Sweden, I received a call which presented a challenge.

Insert # 2 from *It's A Faith Walk!*

Thinking it was the front desk, so it was a complete shock when I heard the voice of The Honorable Minister of Finance in Tonga, Minister Tasi! He shared emails a few times since the days in Tonga, but, his call was a complete surprise!

He was inviting me to extend my stay in Europe instead of returning to America immediately upon my return to London.

Sharing the truth with him about my frequent flyer ticket only being available for the exact day of my return to London (May 15 flying to London and departing London for America), otherwise the return ticket would not be available again for several months (October 15), plus the fact that I could not be stuck in London for several months, so, I trusted they would want to re-schedule the London meetings.

But, he continued to stress the fact that this time frame was critical due to the schedule for the Global Economic Summit. So, I told him I would need to purchase another flight ticket if I was going to be extended in London. He said that would not be a problem since the blessing for their Embassy in London would be of more value than the cost of a flight ticket.

So, I agreed. Then, since I had to know, I asked, *"How did you find a way to call me in Sweden?"*

Minister Tasi was laughing as he said, *"It was easy in Malmo, Sweden, as there is only one Radisson. It was too difficult in Oslo, Norway, as there were many Radissons…"*

While we were talking, God already confirmed I was in Sweden to receive this call and to extend my time in London, so, I agreed to remain in London and assist the Ambassador for the Kingdom of Tonga so the African and Island Nations could receive better standing and recognition within the Global Economic Summit.

A dear woman who was the coordinator for Pastor Harold Dewberry meetings during my first week in Australia met me at the Sydney Airport on my return flight path to fly back to America.

She kept smiling while I shared the brief 'debrief' with her so I had to ask her what she was thinking. She said, *I am amazed that*

228

you are so excited after spending every penny of the blessings during the time in Australia to buy a tick to go to the Kingdom of Tonga.

It surprised me and evidently our Father was surprised, also! The words flowed smoothly during my response, *When GOD provides the opportunity to impact a life and maybe change that life forever, that is a gift! This time, GOD gave me the chance to change a nation and help the leaders choose LIFE!*

Father did not reveal this status to me, until now: *Giving ONE Kingdom a voice resulted in the establishment in 1999 of the G20, a critical point in time when the African and Island Nations were given a voice for the very first time!*

Many testimonies about the days 'DOWN UNDER' while the specific testimony is being revealed to me right now, 20 years later: *Saving a nation!*

WOW ... WOW ... WOW! Training!

That phase of the journey was the plan of GOD when I was offered the chance to go to Tonga with less and one hour notice!

Plus, 20 in Hebrew means: REDEMPTION.

It is the letter Kaph, which means an open hand or palm. It means giving freely with the palm up.

The United Nations had to opportunity to provide REDEMPTION by gathering together the 20, 19 nations and the European Union. However, they chose expand their control and

NOT give a voice to EACH nation, they did give a voice to the nations without a voice prior to 1999!

Definition of G20: *The **G20** (Group of Twenty) is an international forum for the governments and <u>central bank governors</u> from 19 countries and the European Union (EU).*

Prayers for our Father to SEND SOMEONE who will be a voice for Him, a strong voice to the nations regarding the 'control of the centralized banking system' which is NOT good for the people or the nations.

Now, 20 years later – we are hearing from a man who realized the severe levels of the EVIL plan against us – a man who would DECLARE truth about the UN, FAKE NEWS, Planned Parenthood, the Centralized Banking system and the plan against the nation is focused upon ELIMINATING believers in every nation!

Our Father is proceeding through HIS AMBASSADOR(s) with the plan to counter ALL evil! Grateful you are now 'at choice' to become the TRUMP CARD our Father sent to earth 'for such a time as this'. Praying you will say YES!

Remember the WORD shared by Harrison about my life, actually living the life of Joseph not Job. Plus, confirming to me that <u>I agreed with our Father to accept my assignment before I came to earth</u>: ***Whatever it takes to save the nation.***

WOW ... WOW ... WOW. Only after THIS BOOK can I begin to SEE IT & DECLARE IT: *I was sent here, by our Father, for these exact days in HIStory, to do whatever it takes to save this nation.*

This is just being revealed to me while our Father is asking me to insert the specific sections from the Faith Walk book right now. Giving a voice to a nation due to our Father's message, delivered by me, while not realizing I was expressing my voice and because it was a message direct from our Father that is why it mattered.

Forgive me if I do not share any of this in the interviews before the book is 'in hand' because pieces of this testimony are not fair to try and process separate from realizing the depth of the 'full story of walking forward in faith' with our Father!

Father walked me through the desert, the evil plan on earth and never left me, never left me on the side of the road ... never. Looking back, I had the chance to see what life could have been like if I would have chosen a separate path, if I would have been OK with choosing a liberal, make my own future and do my life my way.

While I was in High School, I took on every opportunity to be 'in a school van going to a competition somewhere', singing, playing an instrument, being in a drama production and then I got involved in speech competitions and debate. It was the debate structure which was fully aligned with the liberal structure. In fact, when I was at the tournaments, I was invited to become a member of the Students For A Democratic Society.

Today, the conversation began with a simple statement about an adorable, yet poignant music video on YouTube: The Newfangled Four - A Spoonful of Sugar (parody) [from Mary Poppins]. The song was all about the competition process: RULES – FOLLOW THE RULES. IF you do not follow the rules, your point score goes down!

My friend has an amazing son, Clay. He is in college now but, he was about 11 or 12 when I met him. He gave me a powerful word from the LORD and he knew it was from the LORD! Then, a few weeks later, I asked my friend to check and see if he heard anything else from the LORD. Without hesitation, he said: *Tell her IT'S NOT LIKE turning on a water spigot.*

When we met, Clay was impressed when I told him it was a highlight in my life to be a national debate champion.

In High School, he participated in debate and became a mentor to other debaters. He learned the routine: follow the rules – the rules – the rules our the scoring points during each phase of the debate process go down!

It does not matter what the best option is, what the truth is about the topic, the entire focus is saying what has to be said to win the debate from BOTH perspectives. When she said, *It has changed him* ... Father was prompting me to go back in time 'in that moment' and share how it changed me.

A fact, it was a revelation to me because I completely forgot until this moment when He brought a key fact to my attention: *Invitation at each tournament to join the* Students for a Democratic Society. I did not have any idea what it was about. However, the mention of it was enough to confirm it was not for me.

In the moment, today, Father confirmed it would have taken me on a different path and He wanted me to research the organization. WOW. It was founded by Tom Hayden and Bill Ayers. So much about them was not known until years later.

Reminder for each of us: It is true, true, true ... choose life and know who you follow who you will follow. IF you do NOT know where you are being led, you ARE being led by the Holy Spirit!

Often, people ask about walking in Faith with the Father. It is HUMBLING experience. When we are 'in HIS presence', there are few words to describe what 'standing in awe of HIS majesty' is really like 'in the moment'.

Confirmations of HIS truth are not meant to 'puff us up', they are merely statements which are confirming we are ON or OFF the track of our assignment.

Many more facts and miracles are shared within *It's A Faith Walk!*

To realize the depth of deceit, century after century, devastating many generations … before hearing from a prophet I agreed before I arrived on earth, to do whatever it takes to save the nation … before proceeding with even more intense repentance for any thoughts, words or actions while thinking it should not be like this 'for me' while I am on earth … before our Father confirmed to me that we are EACH here to help it become as Christ taught us to pray that it will become on earth as it is in heaven.

And, the ultimate: Our Father knew the end from the beginning and He knew I would wake up. He knew I would be willing to pay the price to do whatever it takes to get the word to all who have ears to hear and eyes to see the truth. He knew ALL of this before I realize ANY of this.

For years, I said, *I am merely a farmer's daughter from Nebraska. willing to serve …*

While the truth for me is very evident to me, each 'ah ha' moment includes revelation I am to share with believers and that fact is what increases my passion to share the truth each and every day with as many people as possible because our Father has proven to me, *It does not matter who they were before you were with them, it matters who they are because you met them!* He knows me and therefore, He knows I truly know what it is like to NOT be awake!

When I hear from people who say, *My family is not fully awake ... my spouse is not awake ... nobody understands what I am saying.* Often, the best option is to merely BE with them, DEMONSTRATE truth and love to them! This is why Christ said, *...greatest gift is LOVE.*

It shakes them up because the enemy wants us to enter into a conflict and remain divided or on a different path. His plan is clear: divide and conquer. This is why the enemy has pursued so many divisions within the body of believers.

My own sister believes in evolution. I tried diligently to WAKE HER UP. The more I tried, the more I prayed, the more her heart hardened which makes it really tough to be around her! But, by the grace of GOD, I have learned to tell her, *Bless you ... I love you ...* while the spirit operating in her wants to fight me, question me, I only have to remind her she is my sister and I will always love her. All we can do is bring them back to the truth, to the feet of Christ. Then, leave them with our Savior for their life to be 'in HIS hands'. Again, even in our own family, as our Father told me, *If it takes 1000 times of hearing the truth for the heart to turn to Christ, whether we are # 575 or # 999, we may not be the one time of loving someone to witness their salvation choice.*

Hope For Believers

Hope For America

LORD thank You for Your promise! Thank You for providing the angelic vortexes over Macon, Georgia and Moravian Falls, North Carolina 'For The Sake Of America'!

Grateful to know Your hand is upon us and You will never leave us or forsake us! Thank You for providing Your truth in Your word and through Your prophets so we will be prepared to march with You before the SONrise!

For I was humbled when You shared the word with me to share to a special leader in the body of Christ after You provided the same vision of the 'war room', including the same furniture:

"Not enough of my men are preparing and putting on their steel toed boots to march with Me, so I am having to call forth My women, even My widows and My orphans, to prepare My Army to march with Me before the SONrise."

Forgive us LORD for all of the lies shared, all of our misunderstandings passed on generation to generation!

We truly want You to recognize us as Your people who are called by Your name!

Amen (Hebrew meaning, Our GOD is a Faithful KING!)

Life can change in a moment as it did in an area currently called *Ashfall, Nebraska!* Yes. A tropical climate with animals we now find in Africa roamed the plains of Nebraska until the ashes of

236

a Volcano resulted in the 'inability to breathe' while they were on the way to their water hole or they were at their water hole. Amazing to witness 'in person' when you have a chance or you can research it 'on line' as it is a University 'dig' to this day.

The best revelation of this research: Glorious news for me, to realize our Father truly planned to send me to a WARM climate!

To live from glory to glory, it is important to comprehend that our Savior, Jesus Christ, the Messiah, as confirmed in **John 17:22**, gave us the glory that we would be one, united together 'In One Accord' as He and the Father are one. He gave us this truth, while He was with us! Blessings upon you until the next ONE MORE TIME* our LORD brings us together!

Sheila

Email: hisbest4usorders@gmail.com

Ephesians 2:19-22 *We are no longer foreigners and aliens, but fellow citizens... members of God's household, built on the foundation of the apostles and prophets, with Christ Jesus himself as the chief cornerstone. In Him the whole building is joined together and rises to become a holy temple in the Lord. And in Him you too are being built together to become a dwelling in which God lives by His Spirit.*

II Corinthians 12:14-15. (a) *"Now, I am ready to visit you...what I want is not your possessions but you...So I will very gladly spend for you everything I have and expend myself as well."*

II Corinthians 13:11-14. Aim for perfection ... be of one mind, live in peace, and the God of love and peace will be with you. May the grace of the Lord Jesus Christ, and the love of God, and the fellowship of the Holy Spirit be with you all.

* While in Ghana, West Africa for the coronation of a King, Bishop Duncan William's worship team sang a simple verse: ONE MORE TIME, ONE MORE TIME, HE HAS ALLOWED US TO COME TOGETHER ONE MORE TIME, and by the third time they shared this verse, pointing to each other, then, to each of us on the platform and then, to each of the participants speaking at least 13 Afrikaans dialects and nine foreign languages, there was not a dry eye in the house!

Books Authored by Sheila Holm

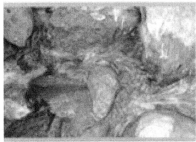

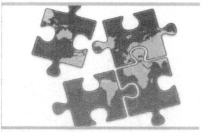

A WAKE UP CALL: IT'S RESTORATION TIME!

MYSTERIES REVEALED: HOW AND WHEN THE CHURCH WAS DECEIVED AND WHAT IS REQUIRED FOR FULL RESTORATION.

SHEILA HOLM

IN SEARCH OF WIGGLESWORTH

A JOURNEY WHICH SPEAKS TO THE VERY CORE OF WHAT IT MEANS TO BE A TRUE BROTHER AND SISTER IN CHRIST!

SHEILA HOLM

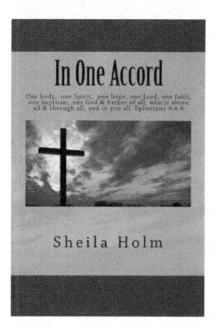

In One Accord

One body, one Spirit, one hope, one Lord, one faith, one baptism, one God & Father of all, who is above all & through all, and in you all. Ephesians 4:4-6

Sheila Holm

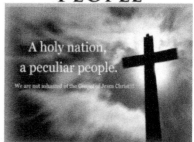

A PECULIAR PEOPLE

A holy nation, a peculiar people.

We are not ashamed of the Gospel of Jesus Christ!!!

DISCIPLESHIP OF PECULIAR PEOPLE BY PECULIAR PEOPLE

SHEILA HOLM

ALWAYS SPEAK LIFE

FOR THE EYES OF THE LORD ARE ON THE
RIGHTEOUS, AND HIS EARS ARE OPEN
TO THEIR PRAYERS ... 1 PETER 3:12

SHEILA HOLM

CHRISTMAS

MYSTERIES UNCOVERED & REVEALED:
TRUTH REGARDING THE BIRTH OF
THE MESSIAH, HIDDEN SINCE 300 AD

SHEILA HOLM

FOR THE SAKE OF AMERICA

AMERICA IS IN TROUBLE
THE ROOT PROBLEMS AND THE
PROMISES OF THE LORD ARE REVEALED
FOR THE SAKE OF AMERICA!

SHEILA HOLM

FOR THE SAKE OF AMERICA II

ANCIENT AND CURRENT ROOTS REVEALED
REPENTANCE FOR DEEPER TRUTH REQUIRED
THEN, THE LORD'S BLESSINGS WILL FLOW AS A
RESTORATION FLOOD FOR THE SAKE OF AMERICA!

SHEILA HOLM

FOR THE SAKE OF AMERICA III

TRUMPET CALL TO AMERICA! DEEPER TRUTH REVEALED.
MORE REPENTANCE REQUIRED FOR FULL RESTORATION.
JOHN 10:27, MY SHEEP HEAR MY VOICE, AND I KNOW THEM,
AND THEY FOLLOW ME, ROMANS 8:14, FOR AS MANY AS ARE
LED BY THE SPIRIT OF GOD, THESE ARE SONS OF GOD.

SHEILA HOLM

Releasing soon

CHOOSING THE 12

WHO INFLUENCE CHOICE

SHEILA HOLM

ALIGN

WITH THE KINGDOM OF HEAVEN

SHEILA HOLM

My Story in HIStory
Sheila Holm

Nation Restoration

Published in 2014

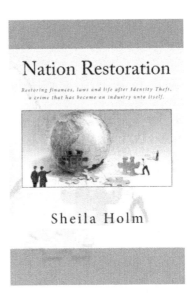

Nation Restoration

Restoring finances, laws and life after Identity Theft, a crime that has become an industry unto itself.

Sheila Holm

FOREWORD BY
KEN BLANCHARD

Seven
Step
Business
Plan

SHEILA
HOLM

"Seven Step Business Plan is the first and only book to provide a simple format for every business to be able to prepare and update their business plan."
— Ken Blanchard,
The One Minute Manager

Seven Step Business Plan

Published, 2007

Latin America edition:

Spanish Language

Published, 2009

ACKNOWLEDGMENTS

AFRICA

Ghana, West Africa

Pastor Sam,

"Truly, GOD has sent you to us with a strong word for our church."

Pastor Charles,

"It blesses my soul to hear of your faith & see the fruit of the ministry."

Johannesburg, South Africa

Pastor Jhanni,

"GOD is doing a good work through you and I pray with you and our church."

Coronation Ceremony

AMERICA

Bishop George Dallas McKinney, California

"**Sheila is GOD's ambassador to encourage Christians, especially pastors, throughout the US, Africa, Australia and Europe. Without sponsors or any visible means of support, she has traveled the world sustained by the faithfulness of GOD.**

Dr. Nancy Franklin, Georgia

"Thank you God for answering my prayers by sending Your apostle to (the region) to unite the believers ... "

Prophetess Nancy Haney, Alaska

"God has never given me this before. I see circles and circles and circles ... you drink and you draw from one circle to the other, and that's what you do, you drink and draw and you bring these circles together ... Pulling many groups together. All these groups need each other ... He can use you for you have ears to hear and you hear His deep truth. You are filtering what is nonsense and what is real ... because you have been in that circle, and because of what you say they are going to merge. It is going to expand, become bigger than you could imagine."

Pastor, Host of "Praise the Lord", TBN,

"...The fruit of the ministry is evident in your testimony..."

Man of God (Georgia), Requesting to be Discipled while attending the coronation of a King in Africa, Georgia

*"...*at my age, it is hard to believe I am learning so much in these few days about what I did not know...realizing what it is to know that I know how it is to live within God's word each day. Will you consider discipling me?"

International Prophet,

"You have remained steadfast to God's plan and God will continue to send you forth for His plan and purpose to be fulfilled, and for the thousands who have not knelt..."

President, Christian Publishing Company

"Only God could orchestrate such a grand plan..."

Prayer Director, International Prayer Center

"God is opening many doors for you..."

Christian Publisher, "God has given you a powerful voice and a sweet spirit..."

Pastor, Southern California

"God is raising you up and sending you forth to many nations..."

International Apostle

"God is doing a mighty work through you, for His righteousness precedes you, showers over you and follows you as a mighty wake. May it continue for each of your days..."

Prophetic Prayer Partner, Minnesota

"Only God could walk you through these days... accomplish so much through you, in the midst of your daily situations, the many blessings shared during each of your travels will continue to shower blessings upon each of the many households around the world..."

AUSTRALIA

Four Square Gospel Church, Aboriginal Cultural Center

Pastor Rex, **"GOD blessed us through your preaching on Easter Sunday. We will never forget that you were in our midst ... GOD brought new people to Jesus today and we thank GOD for what He has done because you answered His call."**

Newcastle, New South Wales, Australia

Pastor Mark, **"...the staff and business leaders heard the message of Personal and Professional Life Management this week, so we are blessed you agreed to preach the word to our church this morning."**

Prayer Team Meeting **"We know now how we will we be able to continue this mighty work when you are not in our midst..."**

ENGLAND

London, England

Pastor Vincent, Glory House, East London, **"...the honor is ours this Easter Sunday."**

Associate Pastor, **"The Glory of our GOD Almighty shines upon you and through you in your speaking and your actions...we give Him praise."**

Protocol Team,

"GOD has mightily blessed us by sending you into our midst."

Pastor Arnold,

"You have blessed the people of this congregation, and in His wisdom and timing, may He bring you back into our midst again, very soon."

Pastor, West London,

"We rejoice with you in hearing and seeing the mighty things GOD is doing."

Pastor, South London, "**Our GOD is evidenced in your life and your speaking, while we continue to thank GOD for the work He is doing through you...**"

High Commissioner, Kingdom of Tonga, serving in the Embassy in London, England; Ambassador Akosita, "**GOD's timing is always right...for you to be with us, prior to the Economic Summit, to meet and pray with us...**"

Sunderland, England

Anglican, Former Church of Pastor Smith Wigglesworth

Pastor Day, "**I thank GOD for sending you to our church this morning, for serving communion to me, and for renewing and restoring me for the call upon my life.**"

Kingdom of TONGA

Pastor Isileli Taukolo, **"Our board and business leaders were fasting and praying and GOD confirmed He was sending someone to us. We are deeply touched by the message GOD sent to us, through you."**

Minister of Finance, Tasi, "**Our meeting was an answer to my prayers, and I thank you for providing the seminar for our senior staff members, and meeting with them individually for prayer and coaching.**"

Government Office, "**Thank you for speaking today and for staying and praying with us.**"

Interpreter, Sela

About the Author

The LORD fulfills upon His promises within the scriptures. He has equipped and trained Sheila while He:

- Places her feet on the soil of each continent,
- Sends her forth without an extra coin or tunic,
- Arranges flights and accommodations in each nation,
- Introduces her before she arrives,
- Lifts her up and encourages her,
- Seats her before governors and kings,
- Fills her as an empty vessel,
- Shares His wisdom and word of knowledge,
- Blesses and heals the people in her path,
- Comforts & re-encourages her to encourage pastors, prophets, apostles, believers, teachers & evangelists,

- Touches people individually in conferences/multitude,
- Speaks through her with power and authority,
- Takes people into gift of laughter when she preaches,
- Addresses situations the body of Christ is facing,
- Unites the people in the region,
- Confirms His word through her with each prayer & message shared,
- Speaks through her so people hear His words in their own language, especially when the translators also experience the gift of laughter and stop translating,
- Directs her path to <u>speak life</u> into each situation whether GOD sends people to her to be re-encouraged or he asks her to pray with a pastor, the church, or someone in a store or a restaurant, etc.

Vision and word *For The Sake Of America* were given to internationally recognized prophets. They were not able to be 'boots on ground' in Georgia so they shared the facts with people they trusted. Then, the vision and word were released to Sheila because she agreed to remain and fulfill upon the assignment after she traveled across country to Georgia for three specific weeks in October 2013. The third message from the man who received the vision and word from Bob Jones activated Sheila to proceed with the research.

Sheila was not aware of the LORD's plan to extend her time from three weeks to three years or that He would reveal such deep truth to her *For the Sake of America!*

She did not realize the LORD would extend her in Georgia for another year while the 'deeper truth' of the ancient and current roots were being revealed to her, one layer at a time. However, the LORD confirmed in a specific vision that He sent her to Georgia because she asked for the assignment.

Since Georgia was not part of her conversations with the LORD she was a bit surprised until the LORD reminded her of her own words each time she witnessed the flow of the body of Christ in other nations He sent her to around the world. She hoped the LORD would send someone to bring the truth to the body of Christ in America.

When the LORD reminded her of her heart's desire, she realized in that moment He sent her to Georgia to be available during this critical time in our nation for His purpose, plan and promise to be made known to the people.

The LORD promised once the Ancient and Current Roots Are Revealed, Repentance of the Deeper Truth is Required. Then, the LORD's Blessings Will Flow As A Restoration Flood *For The Sake Of America!*

She trusted GOD's promise was fulfilled upon. The LORD has continued to provide 'deeper truth' in *For The Sake Of America II* more deeper truth was revealed to her, resulting in *For The Sake Of America III*.

For The Sake Of America IV was not going to be prepared or released. When Sheila asked what the title would be, Father merely stated *For The Sake Of America IV.* She laughed because she was referring to the sub-title as she thought the messages were already provided. When Father told her the sub-title:

God's Trump Card Revealed!

God's Master Plan

Trumps

The Enemy's Master Plan

the outline came together within seven days, and since Father provided the 'title' when she was at an event during Palm Sunday weekend, the book has come together in seven months!

GOD has taken Sheila around the world, church to church, business to business, nation to nation, set her before governors and kings without an extra coin or tunic.

Many confirm she walks in the five-fold ministry. She does not use a title because GOD does the work while He sends her as an apostle and prophet, and He orchestrates all arrangements for her to preach, teach, and evangelize.

People attending the conferences often say her segments are like watching someone walk out of the bible, share for a while and then, go right back in the bible, aka continue upon her journey in HIStory.

Mark Taylor, prophet and author of *Trump Prophecies* has graciously introduced Sheila to McFiles, OmegaManRadio and Sheila Zilinsky Media and the interviews can be found on YouTube.

Made in the USA
Columbia, SC
29 January 2020